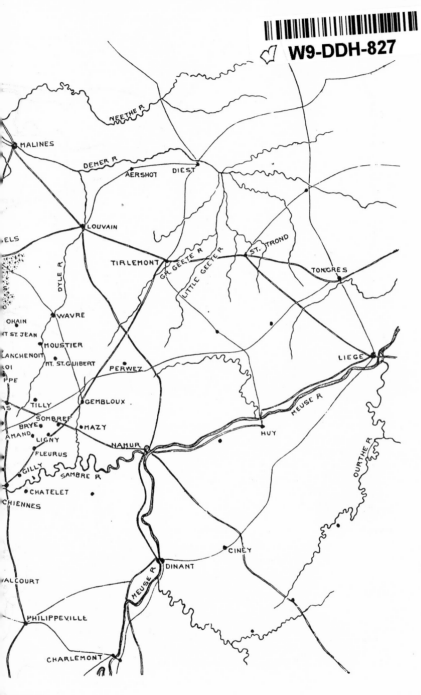

UNTRY

# THE
# CAMPAIGN OF
# WATERLOO

NAPOLEONIC LIBRARY

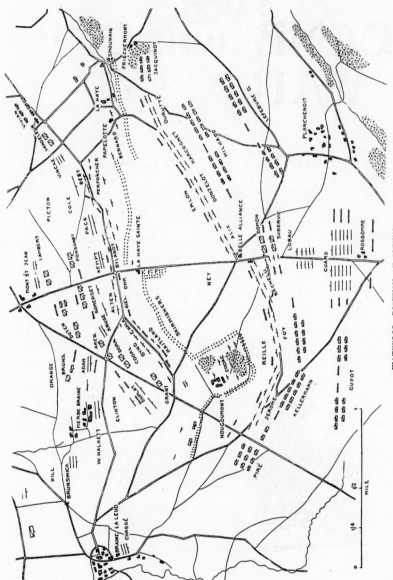

WATERLOO. POSITION AT OPENING

# THE CAMPAIGN OF WATERLOO

## The Hon. J. W. Fortescue

LL. D. Edin.

Greenhill Books

Greenhill
Books

This edition of *The Campaign of Waterloo*
first published 1987 by Greenhill Books,
Lionel Leventhal Limited, 3 Barham Avenue,
Elstree, Hertfordshire, WD6 3PW

This edition and new material
© Lionel Leventhal Limited, 1987

British Library Cataloguing in Publication Data
Fortescue, J.W.
The Campaign of Waterloo. – (Napoleonic Library)
1. Waterloo (Belgium), Battle of, 1815
I. Title   II. Series   940.2'7   DC242
ISBN 0-947898.49-2

Publishing History
*The Campaign of Waterloo* by The Hon. J.W. Fortescue
was first published in 1920 by Macmillan and Co.,
Limited, London, as part of Volume X of *A History of
The British Army*, and for this edition 9 maps and
1 chart have been added from *Napoleon* by Theodore
Ayrault Dodge (Gay and Bird, 1907), and a new index.

**Greenhill Books**
welcome readers' suggestions for books that
might be added to this Series. Please write
to us if there are titles which you would
like to recommend.

Printed by Antony Rowe Limited,
Chippenham, Wiltshire.

# CONTENTS

# CHAPTER I

## HOME AFFAIRS

## RENEWAL OF HOSTILITIES—CAMPAIGN IN THE LOW COUNTRIES

PAGE

# CHAPTER II

## CAMPAIGN IN THE LOW COUNTRIES

# CONTENTS 7

## CHAPTER III

### CAMPAIGN IN THE LOW COUNTRIES

# CHAPTER IV

## Campaign in the Low Countries

## CHAPTER V

## CHAPTER VI

# CONTENTS

# APPENDICES

Officer of King's
Own.

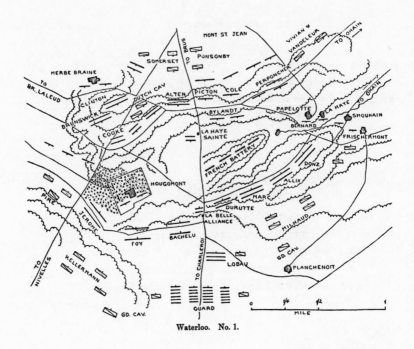

Waterloo. No. 1.

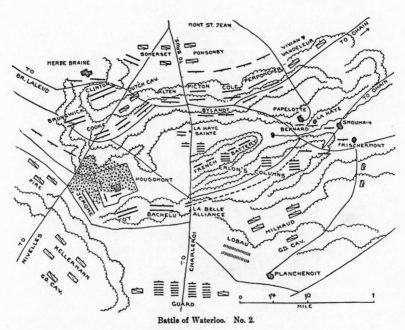

Battle of Waterloo. No. 2.

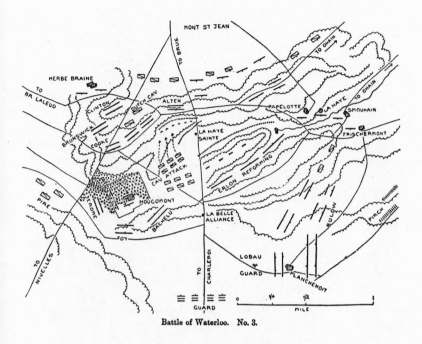

Battle of Waterloo. No. 3.

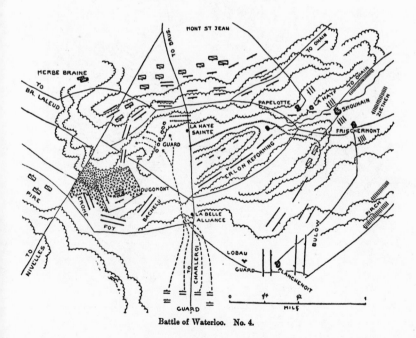

Battle of Waterloo. No. 4.

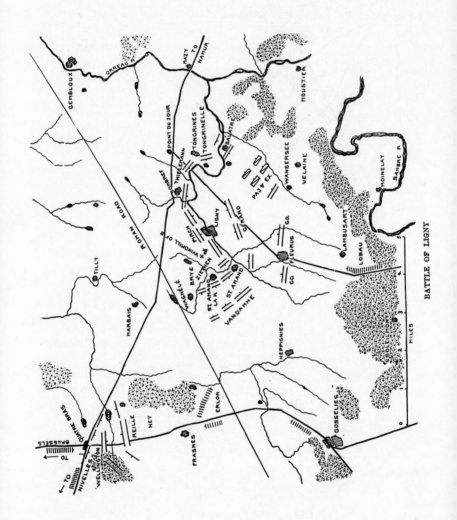

BATTLE OF LIGNY

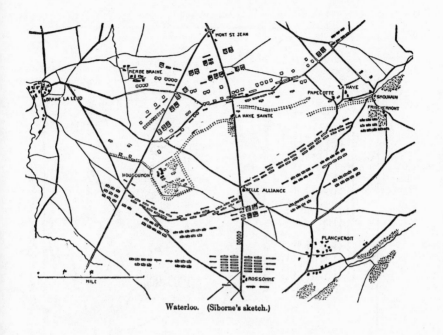

Waterloo. (Siborne's sketch.)

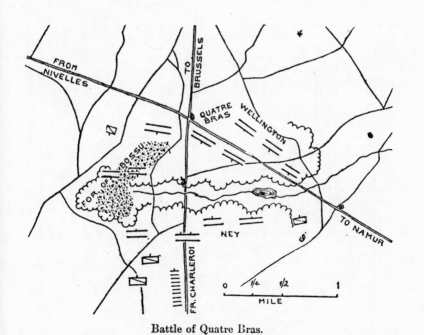

Battle of Quatre Bras.

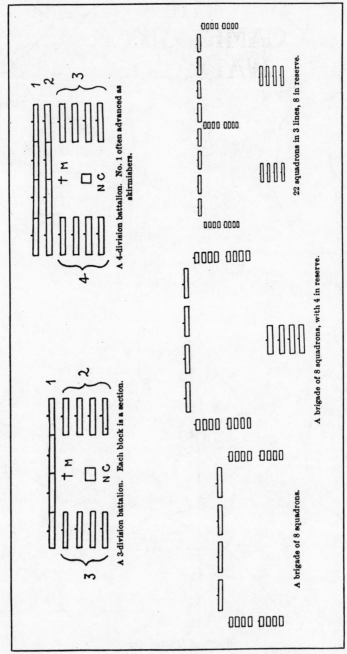

A 4-division battalion. No. 1 often advanced as skirmishers.

A 3-division battalion. Each block is a section.

22 squadrons in 3 lines, 8 in reserve.

A brigade of 8 squadrons, with 4 in reserve.

A brigade of 8 squadrons.

Charts of French Troops Ready to Charge. (From "Maximes de 1815.")

# THE
# CAMPAIGN OF
# WATERLOO

English Dragoon.

# CHAPTER I

NAPOLEON, by sentence of the European Powers, was 1814. conveyed to the island of Elba on the 28th of April 1814 ; and on the 30th of May were signed the Treaties of Paris, which settled for the time, so far as France was concerned, the ambitions and animosities which had arisen out of a quarter of a century of war. Other weighty matters were adjourned until a Congress of the European Powers should meet at Vienna ; but meanwhile France received a slight accession to the territory which she had enjoyed in 1791, and Belgium was united to Holland under the sovereignty of the House of Orange. England for her part retained Malta, Tobago, St. Lucia and Mauritius, and acquired further the conquered colonies of the Cape, Curaçoa and Demerara from the Dutch by purchase. In these circumstances, and until hostilities with America should cease, it was impossible to make very large reductions in the British army. Wellington's battalions were most of them sent away across the Atlantic as fast as they were released from France. The remains of Graham's detachment, with which he had stormed Bergen-op-Zoom, were marched from Holland into Belgium,[1] where they were joined in the course of the summer and autumn by the greater part of the King's German Legion,[2] and by fifteen

[1] 2/1st Guards ; 2nd Coldstream Guards ; 2nd Scots Guards ; 2/25th ; 2/30th ; 33rd ; 2/35th ; 2/37th ; 2/44th ; 2/52nd ; 54th ; 2/69th ; 2/73rd ; 2/78th ; 2/81st ; det. 95th.

[2] That is to say, by all the cavalry, all the Light battalions, five out of seven Line battalions, both horse-batteries, one and a half foot-

1814. thousand Hanoverian Militia. These troops, which in August 1814 were placed under the command of the Prince of Orange, were stationed in the Netherlands under an agreement with Austria, Russia and Prussia, to maintain the provisions of the Treaty of Paris pending the final settlement of Europe by the Congress at Vienna.

The condition of Ireland was anything but peaceful, and it was therefore impossible to disembody the Yeomanry or even the whole of the Regular Militia ; [1] though the Local Militia, under the wording of the Act by which it was created, was disbanded within six weeks of the signature of peace. The only direction in which economy was possible was in respect of the cavalry, the veteran battalions, and the second battalions. In the mounted branch the Household regiments were greatly diminished, and the regiments of the Line were reduced to an establishment of eight troops of sixty men apiece ; and in the infantry before the end of the year eleven veteran battalions, twenty-four second battalions, and ten thousand foreign corps were disbanded. The Artillery was dealt with more summarily, for no fewer than seven thousand men were discharged. Altogether by the close of 1814 forty-seven thousand men had been struck off the strength of the British establishment.[2]

It was not to be supposed that the Opposition in Parliament would quietly acquiesce in the maintenance of so large a military force. Their gloomy forebodings of the past seven years had been steadily falsified ; and, now that Napoleon had been dethroned and peace was at last come, they seized the opportunity offered by Castlereagh's absence at Vienna to offer factious

batteries. There was, however, a good deal of desertion from the Legion. *Wellington Supp. Desp.* ix. 394.

[1] In October there were about 10,000 Militia in Ireland and 6000 in England. *Wellington Supp. Desp.* ix. 368.

[2] Hansard's *Parl. Debates*, xxxi. 587 *seq. Wellington Supp. Desp.* x. 8.

opposition to every measure of the Government.   They 1814.
cavilled at the appointment of the Prince of Orange to
command British troops as " unconstitutional."   They
maintained that it was " unconstitutional " also to disembody a part of the Militia and not to disembody the
whole.   So useful are meaningless epithets to those who
speak for the sake of opposing, and oppose for the
sake of speaking.   Lord Grenville, who ought to have
known better, declared that there was no occasion for
a larger peace-establishment than in 1792.   He, at
least, might have guessed, if not that the Powers who
were rearranging the map of Europe at Vienna were
on the point of flying at each other's throats over the
destiny of Poland, Tuscany and Naples, at any rate
that the weight of England's influence must depend
not a little upon her military strength.   Able but
sentimental gentlemen waxed tearful over the dis-
appointment inflicted upon Genoa by Castlereagh, when
he repudiated Lord William Bentinck's foolish and
unauthorised promises of a new Government after the
model beloved of the Whigs.

The Corn Laws and the Income Tax furnished
more legitimate subjects of criticism ; and, when the
Treaty of Ghent brought the American War to an end
on Christmas Eve 1814, Liverpool was dismayed at
the countenance which the Opposition received from
his own supporters, and entreated Castlereagh to return
home with all haste.   " You might as well expect me to
have run away from Leipzig (if I had been there) last
year to fight Creevy and Whitbread, as to withdraw
from hence until the existing contest is brought to a
point," answered Castlereagh with high contempt ; and
indeed it was intolerable that the ablest of living
English statesmen should be withdrawn from the post
of greatest difficulty to listen to an ignoble adventurer
and a vain, though amiable, chatterbox.   There was,
however, another Englishman at hand to replace him.
Wellington, since the conclusion of peace created a
Duke, had already been entrusted with diplomatic

1815. business in Madrid and in Paris. On the 3rd of February 1815 he relieved Castlereagh at Vienna ; and by the first week in March the Foreign Secretary was again in his place on the green benches. Great was Liverpool's relief. " The country at this moment is peace-mad," he wrote on the 20th of February. "Many of our best friends think of nothing but the reduction of taxes and low establishments ; and it is very doubtful if we could involve the country in a war at this moment for objects which, on every principle of sound policy, ought to lead to it." [1]

The object which, at Castlereagh's request, Liverpool was at the moment contemplating was the expulsion of Murat from the throne of Naples ; the vicinity of Elba to that kingdom being a circumstance which kept King Lewis the Eighteenth and equally Wellington in constant apprehension.[2] The King, indeed, made the state of Italy his excuse for not paying to Napoleon a farthing of the £80,000 which the Allies had pledged him to allow to the fallen Emperor ; and in less than a week after the date of Liverpool's letter, on the night of Sunday the 26th of February, Napoleon embarked by stealth at Porto Ferrajo, with the four hundred men which he retained as his guard, and landed at the Golfe de Jouan on the 1st of March. Moving first upon Antibes he found his overtures repelled by the garrison ; but at Grenoble he was received by the troops with wild enthusiasm, and marched thence with fourteen thousand men upon Paris. Ney, who had set forth to capture his old master, found himself deserted by his best troops and embraced his side ; and on the 20th of March Napoleon entered Paris amid wild shouts of joy from discharged soldiers and from officers who were starving on their half-pay. King Lewis, abandoned by the army, whose work this revolution really was, fled first to Lille and, as his prospects grew worse, was

<hr>

[1] *Wellington Supp. Desp.* ix. 551, 573.
[2] *Ibid.* ix. 503.

for passing over to England, but was persuaded to 1815.
establish his shadow of a court at Ghent. The Duke April.
of Angoulême, who had collected some kind of a
force about Nîmes, with the object of marching on
Lyons and saving at any rate the southern provinces
for the monarchy, gained a trifling success on the
2nd of April, but was surrounded and compelled to
capitulate six days later. On the 16th of April he
embarked at Cette for Spain, and all royalist resistance
to Napoleon in this quarter came to an end.

The Bourbons have been much blamed for their
folly during the first period of their restoration, from
May 1814 till March 1815, and undoubtedly they were
guilty of grave mistakes. But their difficulties, from
the exhausted state of the country, were stupendous ;
and an archangel from Heaven could not have restored
even the beginning of content to France, after all her
misfortunes, within a period of ten months. Yet the
only true supporters of Napoleon's short second empire
were the men who had been discharged in rags and
the officers who had been retired on a pittance, in order
to cover the reconstituted Household troops of France
with gorgeous uniforms.

The news no sooner reached Vienna than the
assembled plenipotentiaries drew up a public declaration that Napoleon Bonaparte had placed himself
outside the pale of public law, and must be delivered
to public justice as a common enemy and disturber
of the peace. To this declaration Wellington, as was
natural, set his hand, and was rewarded by being
denounced by Whitbread in the House of Commons
as one who abetted an openly expressed intention to
assassinate Bonaparte ; an infamous accusation which
might have been excused by Whitbread's ignorance
of the French language, but for which, in his portentous
vanity, he had not the grace to apologise. In every
capital of Europe the alarm was great ; but it was
speedily resolved that the plague should be abated
at any cost. On the 25th of March it was agreed

1815.
March.
between Great Britain, Russia, Prussia and Austria that, pursuant to the Treaty of Chaumont, each of these Powers should place one hundred and fifty thousand men in the field, and not lay down their arms until Bonaparte should have been rendered helpless for war. In the case of Great Britain it was arranged that she should be at liberty to substitute money for men at a fixed rate. Having signed this instrument and a further convention to grant a subsidy of five millions sterling to the contracting parties, Wellington left Vienna on the 29th of March and, travelling at great speed, reached Brussels on the night of the 4th of April. The Prince of Orange had taken alarm from the first. " Bonaparte will, I am persuaded, enter Paris very shortly," he had written on the 17th of March. " He will then move down without delay upon this frontier." Accordingly, he had ordered the fortresses of Western Flanders and Mons to be repaired at once, so as to secure them against a stroke of surprise, and had despatched a messenger to ask for help from General Kleist, then commanding an army of rather over forty thousand Prussians and Saxons, which were stationed about Aix-la-Chapelle. The arrival of Wellington in the Netherlands was an intense relief to Ministers, for the Prince of Orange, with rather absurd conceit, declared that he would not willingly have yielded up his charge to any other man. He was, in fact, burning to invade France and to fight Napoleon single-handed; and, even after receiving from Bathurst strict orders to do nothing so foolish, he had maintained his dispositions for an advance. Young and ambitious of military glory, he was still unaware, though he was shortly to prove, that he was unfit even to command a battalion.[1]

The information that greeted the Duke upon his arrival at Brussels was not of the most cheering. Ten days before quitting Vienna he had urged the re-

[1] *Wellington Supp. Desp.* ix. 593-594, 599, 600, 617-619, 703 ; x. 5. Le Bas, i. 175-179.

inforcement of the army in the Netherlands to the
utmost ; and the answer that awaited him set forth
the following facts.  The entire strength of British
troops which Ministers could immediately place at
his disposal did not exceed six regiments of cavalry
and twenty-five battalions of infantry.  Of these
twenty-five no fewer than fifteen were the " weak
corps and inefficient battalions " which had been
hastily scraped together for the sudden emergency
which called Graham to Holland, and which contained
on an average fewer than five hundred men apiece.
The three battalions of Guards were superior to the
rest in strength, but even they contained four hundred
men too young and weak for service in the field.  Of
the ten new battalions promised to him, the third
battalion of the Fourteenth had not been in existence
two years, and at the outset had been rejected for
active work, the Inspector-general remarking that he
had never seen such a lot of boys, both officers and
men.  The second battalion of the Fifty-ninth were
likewise unfit for any but garrison duties, being young,
half-trained and weak in numbers.  Of the remainder
the first battalions of the Fifty-second, Seventy-first,
and Ninety-first were embarked and sailing for
America, but had been recalled and directed to Ostend ;
while those of the Twenty-third, Fifty-first and Ninety-
fifth were in garrison on the south coast of England.
One and all of these six had served for long in the
Peninsula, though the last three had lost many of
their veteran soldiers owing to the expiration of their
term of service ; and it must be added that the first
battalion of the Fifty-second, by absorbing the remnants of its second battalion, did not add to the number
of units, though it added much to the strength and
quality, of the troops at the front.  The utmost that
Ministers could hope to send, beyond this handful
of men, was a brigade of heavy cavalry and four
battalions of infantry from Ireland, with which the
authorities at Dublin Castle were extremely reluctant to

1815. part, and a battalion of Guards, together with a few
April. squadrons of Household Cavalry as soon as certain
riots, which had arisen in London over the subject
of the Corn Laws, should have subsided. It was
necessary to provide for the safety of Malta, Messina
and Corfu, which would strain the British resources
in the Mediterranean to the utmost ; and in the West
Indies battalions would be required to look after
Martinique and Guadeloupe. In fact, until the return
of troops from America and Canada nothing more
could be done towards the making of a British force
in the Netherlands.[1]

Highly indignant that the British army should be
so poorly represented at so critical a time, Wellington
complained bitterly that the Government might liberate
the soldiers in Ireland at once by calling out the
Militia. But Ministers were unfortunately hampered
by technical difficulties, all of which turned upon the
question, bluntly propounded by Whitbread in the
Commons, "Are we at peace or at war ? " At war with
France England certainly was not and had no wish to
be ; but, on the other hand, she had pledged herself in
concert with the Powers of Europe to suppress Napoleon Bonaparte, who had just arrogated to himself
supreme authority in France and was supported by
the whole of her military forces. Now the Crown
had no right to call out the Militia except in time of
actual war or insurrection. As it happened, there
were still seventeen thousand British Militia, complete
battalions of respectable strength, embodied under
the emergency of the last war which had been ter-
minated by the first Peace of Paris ; and there would
have been more but for the factious clamour of the
Opposition for their immediate disbandment. But of
the disembodied residue so many men, both principals
and substitutes, had taken their discharge on the com-
pletion of their term of service, that not above twenty
thousand were left, and those were dispersed among a

1 *Wellington Supp. Desp.* xi. 6, 19-22.

number of weak battalions.   If those twenty thousand were summoned by reason of a new war, then all the men of the seventeen thousand, whose period of service was bounded by the close of the last war, might reasonably claim their discharge.   All that would be gained therefore by the calling out of the Militia would be the substitution of fifty or sixty weak battalions, counting in all twenty thousand men, for five and twenty or thirty respectable bodies numbering only three thousand less.   Ministers judged the seventeen thousand to be more valuable than the twenty thousand, and beyond doubt they were right.

Moreover, the expediency of a ballot was, in the circumstances, very doubtful.   The country was full of discharged soldiers whom it was most desirable to regain for the regular army ; but there was every probability that, in the event of a ballot, they would engage themselves as substitutes in the Militia, with the hope of receiving later a large bounty to transfer themselves later to the Line.   The whole situation was strangely complicated, so much so that the Cabinet took seven full weeks, dating from Napoleon's entry into Paris, to come to a decision concerning it.   At last, on the 9th of May, they brought forward a Bill to permit the Local Militia to volunteer for duties in garrison, so as to release the old Militia for more important functions.   A fortnight later a second Bill was introduced to draw out and embody the Old Militia itself, the preamble stating that " there was an immediate prospect of war with France "; and it was arranged that the vacancies should be filled by beat of drum, and that a moderate bounty should be offered to old soldiers who would rejoin the regiments of the Line. These two Bills quickly became law on the 14th of June, the day before Napoleon crossed the Sambre, and four days before the battle of Waterloo.[1]

[1] Hansard, xxxi. 223, 265, 653.   Statutes 55, Geo. III. caps. 76, 77. *Wellington Supp. Desp.* x. 66, 83, 183.   *Desp.*, to Bathurst, 6th Apr. 1815.

1815.   It is difficult to understand why Ministers should
April. have waited so long before setting all doubts as to
the Militia Laws at rest by means of the simple
preamble quoted above ; and the whole of this episode
brings into glaring relief the evils of our party system
and the defects of our organisation, even after nearly
a quarter of a century of war, for National Defence.
The eulogists of Napoleon in Parliament had no real
wish to see him again become a menace to Europe,
still less to give him a chance of invading England ;
nor did they even desire their country to lose weight
in the councils of Europe at the Congress of Vienna.
Yet they deliberately laid themselves out to fulfil the
whole of these purposes, simply because by so doing
they might embarrass the Government.   French
authors continue to quote their speeches as evidence
that there was a Napoleonic party in the British Parliament.   There was nothing of the kind ; but there
was a certain number of gentlemen who, finding his
name a useful counter in the game of party, did not
hesitate to degrade it by turning it to that contemptible
use.   They deceived themselves—at least it is charit-
able to believe so—they deceived him, and they caused
considerable anxiety to our General in the field ; thus
accomplishing what is probably the greatest degree
of mischief that is possible to small talkers in their
relation to great men.

As to the vacillation of the Government in regard
to the Militia, it must be remarked that the issue
raised by Whitbread—whether England were at war
or peace — was a real one which troubled even
Wellington at the front long after the words were
spoken in Parliament.   " In the situation in which we
are placed at present," he wrote to the Prince of
Orange on the 11th of May, " neither at war or at
peace, unable on that account to patrol up to the
enemy and ascertain his position by view or to act
offensively upon any part of his line, it is difficult if
not impossible to combine our operations because there

are no data upon which to found a combination." 1815.
Yet the British Navy had begun to take French prizes April.
in the Channel and on the Atlantic seaboard before
the end of March.   The Prince of Orange had arrested
French prisoners who were on their way to France
from Russia ; and the Continental Powers had cut off all
regular communications between France and the world
without.   All of these were hostile acts, and it is
therefore difficult to understand why Ministers should
have boggled at the wording of the Militia Statutes.
But be it observed that, if our system of National
Defence had been based upon the compulsory personal
service of every man of military age, the difficulty
arising from the wholesale discharge of substitutes
would not have arisen.   It would have been sufficient
to call out the Militia, and the ranks would automatic-
ally have been full of trained men.   No system of
National Defence is sound which recognises, as the
British system had always recognised, the principle of
substitution.

To return to Wellington's army, cavalry, from the
nature of the American War, was more easily provided
than infantry ;  and the Horse Guards had made no
difficulty about the immediate despatch of six regiments of Light Horse which had served in the Peninsula.   But the whole of them were weak and could
send abroad only three squadrons apiece, of fewer than
one hundred and fifty of all ranks to the squadron.
The Artillery was in a still more woeful plight.   There
was plenty of guns and ammunition ;  but, since seven
thousand of the Royal Regiment had been discharged
since the Peace of Paris, the Master-general could
provide neither men nor horses.   Considering the
difficulty of training gunners and drivers, this immediate and sweeping reduction of the Artillery,
before the Congress of Vienna had concluded its
labours, was reckless in the extreme ;  but there the
fact was.   Wellington asked for one hundred and fifty
cannon, and the Master-general was unprepared to

1815. supply immediately more than forty-two.   Nor could
April. he hope to furnish drivers, except by enlisting post-
boys for short periods, so as to make use of those who
were out of place, and by offering four guineas bounty
to such Hanoverians as might condescend to accept it.[1]

Over and above the British troops, and almost to
be considered as a part of them, was the King's German
Legion, some corps of which had been halted in the
Netherlands while on their way to Hanover for disbandment.   They comprised five strong regiments of
cavalry, eight weak battalions of foot, and three and a
half batteries of artillery with thirty guns, of which
four corps of the horse, five of the foot, and three of
the artillery had served under Wellington in the Peninsula.   Supplementary to the Legion were the Hanoverian Militia, consisting of one battery, two regiments
of cavalry, and twenty-five battalions of infantry.
These were all of them young half-trained troops, and
greatly deficient in officers.   As the regiments of the
Legion were in want of men, Wellington proposed
that they might be filled up, as in England, by volun-
teers from the Militia ; but, this suggestion being
rejected by the Hanoverian Government, he had no
alternative but to reduce the battalions of the Legion
from ten companies to six, and to transfer the super-
numerary officers and non-commissioned officers from
the Legion to the Militia.   This was a false policy,
for it is easier to make good infantry by mixing young
soldiers with twice their number of veterans, than by
keeping the young soldiers together and adding only
an infusion of old officers and sergeants ; but the
Hanoverians decreed that this mistake should be
deliberately made, and made it was.[2]

As regards the Staff, Wellington complained bitterly
that he was flooded with officers who were all of them
useless.   " I might have expected," he wrote, " that

[1] *Wellington Supp. Desp.* x. 18, 183.
[2] *Wellington Desp.*, to the Prince Regent, 17th April 1815.
Beamish, ii. 323 *n*.

the Generals and Staff formed by me in the last war would have been allowed to come to me again, but instead of that I am overloaded with people I have never seen before ; and it appears to be purposely intended to keep those out of my way whom I wished to have." As the Duke repeated statements to this effect at intervals to the end of his life, it will be well to examine the matter more closely. It must be premised that the Anglo-Hanoverian force which he took over from the Prince of Orange was an organised army with its staff complete ; and it will be admitted that, while it is easy to give a general a free hand in nominating his staff when every place is vacant, it is difficult, without hardship, to do so when many places are already filled up by officers who have held their posts for many months. Nevertheless the Duke of York, through Sir Henry Torrens, desired Wellington, immediately after his arrival in the Low Countries, to favour him with his wishes respecting all appointments; and Torrens himself not only wrote at once to recall Sir George Murray, who had sailed to Canada to take the place of Prevost, but privately begged the Field-marshal not to hesitate, on the score of friendship, to displace a relative of his own, an old Peninsular officer, from the Quarter-master-general's department. To make things still easier, Torrens repaired to the Netherlands himself to facilitate the arrangement of these and kindred matters.

The Quarter-master-general to the Prince of Orange was Sir Hudson Lowe, an officer of great ability, deep professional knowledge, and very wide experience, having been present at thirteen general actions in which Napoleon in person was commanding the French. Torrens speedily discovered that Lowe " would not do for the Duke " ; and it was arranged that Sir Hudson should take his departure immediately upon Murray's return, and that Colonel de Lancey should be summoned to resume his old place as Deputy Quarter-master-general. De Lancey demurred to the

1815. "indignity" of returning to a situation which he had
April. so long held in the Peninsula, but presently set out
for Brussels ; and the removal of Lowe to a command
in the Mediterranean at the end of May left De
Lancey in the post, which he had desired, of Chief
Staff Officer. The Adjutant-general was Sir Edward
Barnes, one of Wellington's brigadiers in 1813 and
1814 and an excellent man for the place. The head
of the Artillery was Colonel George Wood ; the head
of the Engineers Sir James Carmichael Smyth, who
had worked out the plans for the very able attack on
Bergen-op-Zoom ; and the Commissary-general was
Mr. Dunmore, who had been specially sent for from
the Peninsular Army by Graham.

The divisional commanders were George Cooke, who
had for some time been in charge of Cadiz and had
served throughout Graham's campaign in Holland,
Vandeleur, Charles Alten, and Hinüber, all of whom
Wellington had known well in the Peninsula, and
Victor Alten, of whom Wellington had rid himself.
The brigadiers were Peregrine Maitland, who had
already served with the Duke in the Pyrenees ;
Lyon, who had commanded a battalion in Portugal
until 1812 and since then a division of Hanoverians
at Göhrde ; Kenneth Mackenzie, a pupil of Charles
Stuart and of John Moore, who had distinguished
himself in various campaigns ; Frederick Adam, whose
fortunes, unluckily for him, had been linked to John
Murray and William Bentinck ; Colin Halkett,
Ompteda, Arentschild, Bussche, Dörnberg, and Du
Plat, all of the German Legion, of whom the first four
were veterans of the Peninsula and the last two alone
bore unfamiliar names. In the case of Adam, the
Duke of York represented that he was an intelligent
and distinguished officer to whom a brigade had been
long promised, and that, as he chanced to be in the
Netherlands, he had been placed upon the staff of
the army there. Yet another brigadier, Johnstone,
was in command of the brigade which was on the point

of starting for America when it was recalled and sent
to Flanders ; and it was reasonably thought unjust
that he should be removed solely on account of the
change of destination. So far, therefore, it does not
appear that Wellington had any just grievance against
the original composition of the staff of the army in
the Netherlands ; and it may be added that the first
new names added to the list by the Duke of York
were those of Hill, Colville, Clinton, and Vivian.

Passing next to the junior members of the Prince
of Orange's staff, two out of five in the Adjutant-
general's department had served on the staff of the
Peninsular Army with distinction from beginning to
end ; a third, after brilliant work as a regimental officer,
had joined the staff in 1813 ; a fourth had commanded
a battalion under Graham, and the fifth had been a
staff-officer in the West Indies. In the Quarter-
master-general's department, one of the four deputies
had served in that same department from the first to
the last of the Peninsular War, two more had passed
through the war partly as regimental and partly as
staff-officers, and the fourth, having been attached to
Lord Cathcart while that nobleman was Commissioner
with the Russian armies in 1813 and 1814, could
claim at least a considerable experience of work in the
field. As the whole of these gentlemen retained their
places, there seems to have been no great objection to
them. When Wellington took over the army,
eighteen new officers were added to the Adjutant-
general's department and twenty-four to the Quarter-
master-general's. Among the former are to be found
the familiar names of Elley and Waters ; and, so far as
I can ascertain, nearly all of the remainder had seen
service in the Peninsula, more than one of them on
the staff. There is only one whose appointment
suggests itself to me decidedly as a job. Among the
latter are to be found Felton, Hervey, Jeremiah
Dickson, Lord Greenock, Gomm and four more who
had done the like work in the Peninsula and were men

1815.
April-
May.
of tried capacity; and of the residue some certainly, and many probably, had learned at least their regimental duty in Spain and Portugal.

For the rest, the Duke of York was ready and indeed eager to send out Edward Paget, Dalhousie, Picton and Cole. Kempt, Pack, Byng, and William Ponsonby were on their way to the Low Countries. Alexander Dickson was sent out specially to do any work with the artillery that Wellington might choose to assign to him. Colquhoun Grant was spared to take charge of the department of intelligence ; and McGrigor, though about to take up the duty of Director-general of Hospitals, offered to come over to head-quarters and organise the medical service. In fact, of Wellington's most trusted subordinates only Murray and Burgoyne were absent, both of them in America. Altogether, although there was undoubtedly some friction in the matter of appointments to the staff, and there may have been more young gentlemen than work could be found for, it seems to me that, except in the matter of reducing its numbers, Wellington had his own way and had no right to complain that his staff was without experience. The secret of all his ill temper seems to have been that many of his former staff-captains and majors had, by exchange into the Guards, obtained the rank of lieutenant-colonel, and were on that account at first rejected by the Duke of York, though subsequently permitted to take up their appointments. Wellington's sweeping statements therefore, on this as on some other topics, should not be accepted without much reservation.[1]

It remains to consider the Allied armies with which Wellington was expected to act, both within his own command and without it. Of the Dutch troops

---

[1] *Wellington Supp. Desp.* x. 1-6, 9-11, 24, 43, 78-79, 84, 130, 219; Despatches to Torrens, 21st, 28th April, 5th May; to Maj.-Gen. Darling, 2nd May; to Lord Stewart, 8th May; to Dr. Renny, 22nd May, 1815. *Life of Sir William Gomm*, p. 348.

the reports sent to him were contradictory. In general their spirit was said to be good ; but many of the officers of all grades, as well as some of the men, had been in the service of France, and were suspected to be, not unnaturally, in sympathy with her.   The bond of military comradeship is strong ;  and the French faction in Holland, notwithstanding its defeat by the bold diplomacy of Sir James Harris in 1787, had by no means been wholly extinguished.   At the head of the Ministry of War was General Janssens, who, having fought unsuccessfully against the British both at the Cape and in Java, would hardly have been human if he had felt kindly towards them ;  and the officers of almost every department under him were known to be at heart partisans of the revolution and of France.   The exception among them was the Quarter-master-general, Major-general Constant de Rebecque, a loyal, able, and energetic officer, who had accompanied the Prince of Orange throughout the campaigns in the Peninsula.   The army itself was in course of re-organisation ;  the Dutch fortresses were in bad order ; and there was a scarcity of muskets.

The Belgian troops were represented, unequivocally and not inaccurately, to be bad and untrustworthy. The creation of the army for the service of the King of the Netherlands had only begun in February 1814, and had been greatly hampered by want of funds, clothing and arms, with the inevitable consequence of much desertion.   The officers were said to be friendly to the French, but the general attitude of the privates, and indeed of the whole population, was that of sulky indifference.   In 1814, when the Belgians had received a promise of independence, they had rejoiced over their deliverance from the yoke of Napoleon.   But when they found their country annexed to Holland, by no will of their own but for the convenience of the mightier powers, they were filled with disgust towards European politics, and regarded with impartial hatred all the contending

1815.
April-
May.

nations which were preparing once again to turn their fair and unhappy land into an arena for the settlement of their differences. There was no lack of brave men of all ranks among them ; they had proved their courage when fighting under the standards of Napoleon; but they had no enthusiasm for the new cause for which they found themselves impressed, and they saw in it nothing worth the spending of their blood. An impartial observer is bound to admit that they were amply justified. Since the Belgians were of this stamp and the Dutch troops were mostly militia, it was very doubtful whether they would be of great military value, whatever their appearance. Wellington after inspecting them pronounced on them the following judgment. The Nassauers (it will be remembered that a battalion of them had deserted to the British in France) were excellent ; the Dutch Militia were a very good body of men, though young ; the Belgians were young and, some of them, very small, but well clothed and equipped and, apparently, well disciplined ; the cavalry were well mounted but indifferent riders. In his heart, however, the Duke expected little of them, and he would gladly have imported ten thousand of the Portugese who had fought, generally, well for him in the Peninsula ; but his effort to obtain them met with no success.[1]

Altogether the Duke was within the bounds of moderation when he described his army as infamous. Nevertheless, though his British troops were for the most part far inferior to any that he had seen in the field since 1794, they, together with the King's German Legion, were his most trustworthy soldiers ; and he considered it imperative so to mingle them

[1] *Wellington Supp. Desp.* x. 15-17, 167; and see Le Bas, *La Campagne de 1815*, i. 34, 35 ; and James, *Campaign of 1815*, pp. 18, 19. I am afraid that not all the pleading of Le Bas and his collaborator can satisfy me that the Dutch and Belgians were good troops and ready to fight the French. It would be contrary to human nature if they had been ; and it is no reproach to them, or at any rate to the Belgians, that they were not.

with the rest as to impart some measure of stability
to the whole.    In this, however, as in every design
which he framed for the organisation and disposition
of his forces, he was at the outset thwarted by the King
of the Netherlands.    This Prince was the son of the
Stadtholder who had taken refuge in England in 1795
and had died there in 1806.    Unlike his father, he
lacked neither intelligence nor good intentions, and
was by no means without experience of military
operations in the field.    His new position as Sovereign
of the Netherlands made, as the British Cabinet
recognised, the choice of advisers and administrators
very difficult; for he was confronted with the alternatives
of employing men of ability and weight but of doubtful
loyalty, owing to their former connections, or men of
unimpeachable principles but lacking both knowledge
and authority.    Some of the most important of those
whom he actually selected were viewed by Wellington
with profound distrust ;  and to their influence he
ascribed the steady opposition of the King to all
measures which he recommended.    It is likely enough
that the Duke was right ; for the story of British
statesmen from 1688 to 1714 and of Napoleon's
marshals in 1814 and 1815 shows that, where there
are rival dynasties, men generally seek to be on good
terms with both.    On the other hand, it must be
admitted that some of the British demands were
calculated to wound the susceptibilities and excite the
suspicion of good Netherlanders, most notably that
which required Ostend and Antwerp, the keys of the
British communications, to be entrusted to British
commanders.    Still, the Dutch had no one but themselves to thank if the Cabinet in Downing Street was
wary in dealing with them.    No people could have
shown a more wretched spirit in 1793, 1799 and 1814,
when the red-coats had landed to help and hearten
them to the reconquest of their independence ;  and
too much blood and treasure had already been sacrificed
in reliance upon that " rising of the Dutch " which

1815.
April-
May.

was always promised and never fulfilled.    The Hollanders professed to mourn over the freedom of which Napoleon had bereft them ; but it was when they thought of their lost commerce that they wailed loudly and from their hearts.

Each party therefore watched carefully for foul dealing in the other ; and Wellington, who with all his faults was at least a straightforward man, read treachery in every obstacle raised by the King against his wishes.   Perhaps the Duke hardly made allowance for the exaltation which kingship might produce upon a potentate who, up to the past twelvemonth, had possessed neither territory nor subjects.   A sense of the ridiculous is not too common in royal families.   The Prince of Orange had with difficulty been restrained from invading France in order to measure his military genius against Napoleon's ;  and his father may well have thought that a crown adds an augmentation to the brain as well as an adornment to the brow.   However that may be, the contention between the King and the Duke became so hot that Wellington on the 4th of May shook the dust off his feet and sent a message to the effect that, unless His Majesty mended his ways, the British Commander would have nothing more to do with him.   On the same day the King made over to him with no ill grace the command of the whole of his troops, with the rank of Field-marshal in the service of the Netherlands.[1]

This difficulty surmounted, the Duke distributed his army into three corps.   The First, commanded by the Prince of Orange, consisted of the First and Third British Divisions under Cooke and Charles Alten, the 2nd and 3rd Netherlands Divisions under Generals Perponcher and Chassé, and a Dutch Division of Cavalry under General Collaert.   The Second, under Lord Hill (as we must now call him), was made up of the Second and Fourth British Divisions under Clinton and Colville, the 1st Netherlandish Division

[1] *Wellington Supp. Desp.* x. 167, 218, 222.

under General Stedman, and a Netherlandish brigade 1815.
under General Anthing, the whole of the Netherlanders April-
being subject to Prince Frederick of Orange, aged May.
eighteen.  The Third Corps, or Reserve, was composed
of the Fifth and Sixth British Divisions, which were
ultimately commanded by Picton and Lambert (for
Cole had married a wife and therefore could not come
in time for the opening of the campaign), the Nassau
contingent of three battalions, the cavalry-divisions of
the British and of the King's German Legion (com-
prehending sixty-nine squadrons in seven brigades,
with six batteries of horse-artillery), twelve squadrons
of Hanoverian cavalry, and three brigades of Netherlandish cavalry with one battery of horse-artillery.
To the Brunswick contingent of eight battalions, four
squadrons and two batteries were in due time to be
added, for the most part young and raw troops, but
steady enough in the cause of the Allies.

But this list by no means exhausts the details of the
intermingling.  In every British Division except the
First, foreigners were blended with red-coats.  Alten's
and Clinton's had each one brigade of British, one of
the Legion, and one of Hanoverians ; Picton's and
Colville's had each two brigades of British and one of
Hanoverians ; Lambert's comprised one brigade of
British and one of Hanoverians.  Even so, however,
the subtlety of mixture is not yet wholly expressed.  In
Cooke's division of Guards the three young battalions
were stiffened by one old one from the Peninsula.  In
Alten's, where all the British were young, the battalions
of the Legion were veterans and the Hanoverians were
regulars ; in Colville's, where the British were both
old and young, the Hanoverians were both regulars
and militia ; in Clinton's, Picton's and Lambert's,
where the British as well as the troops of the Legion
were old, the Hanoverians were all militia.  In like
manner the Prince of Orange had been careful to mix
up regular battalions with militia and Belgians with
Dutch.  Well might Wellington doubt the quality of

1815. his army and pronounce that its organisation, together
April- with the choice of officers, was a matter of great
May. difficulty.

By extreme good fortune the extension of Prussian
territory to the extreme west had brought about the
presence of some thirty thousand Prussian troops and
fourteen thousand Saxons, under General Kleist, upon
the Lower Rhine. This force was to be completed
to five corps with a joint strength of a hundred and
twenty thousand men, the whole to be commanded by
Blücher, with Gneisenau for the chief of his staff.
The number sounded imposing, but the quality of
the troops left much to be desired. Nearly half of
the infantry—sixty-six out of one hundred and thirty-
six battalions—was composed of militia and, of these
sixty-six, twenty-four were of new formation and in-
cluded six from Westphalia, which had only since
the Peace been placed under Prussian rule. Of the
seventy battalions of the Line two were from the
Duchy of Berg, the appanage of Murat under Napoleon,
and had served in the French Army ; and there were
among the rest eight thousand recruits levied in the
newly acquired provinces between the Rhine and the
Meuse. The clothing, equipment and armament of
all were equally defective, there being in some regiments
muskets of three different calibres, and no uniformity
of belts or pouches. The cavalry was in worse
condition even than the infantry. The regiments of
the Line numbered twenty against fifteen of militia ;
but, of the twenty, one half were of recent creation,
and, of the fifteen, two had only just been scraped
together. The artillery was well provided with guns
but short of gunners—in fact in precisely the same
state as the British. Blücher, the Commander-in-
Chief, was a fine fighting soldier, full of activity in
spite of his seventy-one years, rough and illiterate but
staunch and shrewd, and not in the least afraid of
Napoleon. Gneisenau, who was supposed to make
good what Blücher lacked in brains, enjoyed a great

reputation as a scientific officer and a profound strategist, but did not shine in other capacities, being a timid commander and an indifferent tactician. Un- aware of his defects, or at any rate unwilling to admit them, he conceived himself to be undervalued, and vented his spleen in querulousness, jealousy and suspicion ; and, though he hated the French, he did not love the English. His talents, however, when added to the peculiar qualities of Blücher, made a very powerful combination.

Let us now turn to Napoleon and take notice of the force that he could match against these two very poor armies of Wellington and Blücher. The France to which he returned was not the France which he had left behind him in 1814 ; and he presented himself to the nation not as Emperor, but as First Consul, the leader of a revolution which was to overthrow the evils restored by the Bourbons and deliver the people from the tyranny of priests and kings. The remnant of the old revolutionists was inclined to take him at his word and repeat the violence and outrage of 1793 ; but, once reinstalled at the Tuileries, Napoleon's innate loathing for the mob reasserted itself, and he began forthwith to resume the pomp and outward trappings of the Empire as if he were once more absolute. Here, however, he was checked. Moderate as well as extreme men exclaimed against a despotism and clamoured for a liberal constitution ; and, unless he were prepared to make himself a mere chief of revolutionary banditti, he was bound to give way. In truth his return was not very welcome except to his old companions in arms. The heads of the provincial administration, though half of them had been nominated by him and continued in their places by the Bourbons, showed no zeal in his cause. Their underlings were actively unfriendly ; and an attempt to get rid of them by a new election had no effect but to reinstate them with greater influence. The permanent civil service contained many adherents of

King Lewis.  The clergy were naturally irreconcil-
ably hostile.  In La Vendée there was from the end
of April a renewal of insurrection.  Everywhere it
was realised that the Empire signified war, whereas
the entire nation longed for peace.  The funds,
having fallen with a rush from 78 to 58 within less
than a month, continued to sink slowly through May
and June ; and no efforts of Napoleon could arrest
them.  He quickly produced a constitution, more
liberal than that granted by the Bourbons, which
bewildered many and pleased none ; and he appointed
the 1st of June for its solemn ratification by the people.

Even in dealing with the troops he was cautious
of exercising arbitrary power.  The Army of Lewis
the Eighteenth numbered slightly over two hundred
thousand men, but Napoleon dared not double its
strength by such measures as had been the rule under
the Empire.  There were something over one hundred
thousand more men who were on leave or who had
taken leave, or, in plain English, deserted ; and it
was reckoned that sixty thousand of these could be
recovered.  The Emperor, however, delayed to call
them to the colours until he had sent a circular to the
powers of Europe making proposals for a peaceful
settlement.  This missive was returned unopened by
the Prince Regent of England and rejected with as
little ceremony by the rest.  The summons was
meanwhile issued, and seventy-five thousand men
responded to the call.  Voluntary enlistment produced
fifteen thousand more, and the enrolment of the
seamen at the national dockyards added yet another
six thousand.  At the end of June, moreover, Napoleon
hardened his heart to conscribe the men due for
service in 1815, some of whom had already served
under him in 1814 ; and within a week nearly fifty
thousand of them were assembled in the various
departmental centres.  Besides these there were at
his disposal the National Guard, consisting of some
two hundred thousand men between the ages of

twenty and sixty, and capable of expansion to more than ten times that number. Of these he ordered for the present the mobilisation of some two hundred and thirty thousand ; and, notwithstanding recalcitrance in some quarters, one hundred and fifty thousand were at their appointed stations, in fortress or in camp, by the second week of June. With them, five and twenty thousand veterans and sundry local corps sufficed for the guarding of strong places and frontier-roads.

Thus there was a fair prospect that half a million French would be more or less ready for the field by August ; but small arms and cartridges were scarce and, though there was abundance of cannon, carriages and ammunition were deficient. Moreover the magazines were empty, the clothing of the existing troops was in rags, and both cavalry and artillery were very short of horses. With his usual energy and resource the Emperor set himself to remedy these defects and to repair the fortifications ; and being ably seconded by Davoût, whom he had placed in charge of the Ministry of War, he achieved an astonishing measure of success. The order for mobilisation had hardly been issued before the indefatigable brain had sketched the organisation of the force, which was altered at the end of May into its final form—an Army of the North, one hundred and twenty-four thousand men, under Napoleon's own command ; an Army of the Rhine, twenty thousand men, under Rapp ; another of the Alps, twenty-four thousand men under Suchet, with subsidiary corps, amounting together to fourteen thousand men, in support ; and two corps of the Eastern and Western Pyrenees, fourteen thousand men, under Decaen and Clausel. The greater number of his generals rallied to him ; but a few stood aloof, and a few more, though willing, were rejected. Of the Marshals, Victor, Marmont and Berthier, who had followed Lewis to Belgium, were struck off the list, and Augereau with them. Oudinot, Gouvion St. Cyr, and Kellermann were left severely alone ;

Masséna and Macdonald were pressed to accept commands but refused them. Berthier, who was at Bamberg when Napoleon left Elba, was anxious to return to France, but was denied a passport. On the 1st of June he fell, apparently by accident, from a window on the third floor of his house to the pavement below, and was picked up dead. Soult, therefore, was installed as Chief of the Staff, a position for which his great military talents, impaired as they were only by his irresolution on the battle-field, seemed particularly to qualify him. In the Army of the North, which was distributed into five corps, the generals of Spain were again prominent, the first corps being assigned to d'Erlon and the second to Reille. The three that remained were allotted to Vandamme, Gérard and Mouton, Count Lobau. Drouot took charge of the Imperial Guard and Grouchy of the cavalry.

There is still a name wanting from the list of Napoleon's greatest lieutenants, that of Joachim Murat, King of Naples. On the eve of his escape from Elba Napoleon had sent him a message, bidding him prepare for war, since, if the Austrians declared against the revival of the French Empire, the Neapolitan army would be required for an important diversion against them. At the outset Murat declared to the Ministers at Vienna that his policy should be subordinated to that of the Emperor Francis; but, fearing lest Napoleon might re-annex Italy, he prepared to conquer Italy for himself. On the 29th of March he moved his army from Ancona towards Bologna. Then crossing the line of demarcation between Austrian and Italian territory, he advanced to Rimini, and on the 30th published a proclamation calling all Italians to arms for the freedom and unity of their country. Advancing next to Bologna, from which the Austrians fell back before him, he on the 4th of April occupied Ferrara, Modena and Florence. There his progress was stayed. The Austrians, having gathered in force behind the Po, repelled all his efforts to cross the

river, and taking the offensive thrust him back to
Ancona.  The decisive battle was fought on the 2nd
and 3rd of May, which left him a week later with only
ten thousand of the forty thousand men with which
he had begun the campaign.  On the 19th he fled
from Naples to Toulon, from whence he sent a letter
to Napoleon asking for a command in his army.
Napoleon, sufficiently vexed that his only ally in Europe
should have spent his strength in a mad enterprise
which could profit no one except his enemies, rejected
the overture in harsh terms ; and therewith vanished
all hope that Murat would take his old place at the
head of the French cavalry.

1815.
April-
May.

Various plans of campaign were produced from
the various capitals of the powers, but were finally
reduced by Schwarzenberg to one.  According to this,
France was to be invaded by six armies simultaneously.
On the extreme right, that is to say in the north,
Wellington with ninety to a hundred thousand men
was to advance between Maubeuge and Beaumont ;
on the left of Wellington the Prussians under Blücher,
rather under one hundred and twenty thousand men,
were to penetrate between Philippeville and Givet ;
on the left of Blücher one hundred and fifty thousand
Russians under Barclay de Tolly were to enter by
Sarrelouis and Saarbrück ;  and on the left of de Tolly
two hundred thousand Austrians and South Germans
were to break in by Sarreguemines and Bâle ;  and the
whole of them were to converge by Péronne, Laon,
Nancy and Langres upon Paris.   On the extreme south
fifty thousand Austrians and Piedmontese from Upper
Italy, and twenty-five thousand more Austrians, who
were opposed to Murat, were to cross the Alps and
turn right and left upon Lyon and Provence.   In
their usual leisurely fashion the Austrians set down
the opening of the campaign for the end of June or
beginning of July, since they and the Russians could
not count upon being complete and in readiness at
an earlier date.   Meanwhile, of course, the armies of

1815. Wellington and Blücher were to form the outposts of
April- the entire host, so as to cover the general concentration
May. on the eastern frontier of France.

Wellington, and for that matter Blücher also, were
strongly opposed to delay and anxious to take the
offensive as soon as possible, so as to check, or at any
rate to embarrass, the re-establishment of Napoleon's
authority by showing the French people the disastrous
consequence of accepting it. Wellington also insisted
particularly upon the importance of preventing
Napoleon from gathering any headway outside the
boundaries of France. The great Emperor's system
was, so far as possible, to support his armies at the
expense of his enemies, to make war, as Wellington
put it, a pecuniary resource ; and the Duke had truly
foretold in the Peninsula that, as soon as hostilities were
transferred to the soil of France, the zeal of the French
soldiers and inhabitants would very quickly languish.
Again, a triumphal entry, bloodless or the reverse, into
Belgium, would certainly rally the Belgians, and probably the Dutch also, to Napoleon ; and the moral
effect in Europe would be very great. The new King
of the Netherlands had just set up his capital at
Brussels. The restored King of France had taken
refuge at Ghent. If both of these potentates were
forced to take to their heels because the Allies from
want of energy or alleged military reasons were unable
to protect them, the old legend of Napoleon's invinci-
bility would be re-established and his partisans would
show their heads all over Europe. In England, for
instance—and this was what Wellington particularly
dreaded—the existing Ministry might be driven from
office with the full assent of their former supporters,
now become " peace-mad," and would be replaced by
such men as Grey, Whitbread and Tierney, hungry
for office after twenty years of exclusion, strongly
possessed by the false beliefs which they had been
proclaiming for years, and practically committed to
a reversal of the Government's policy, not because

it was wrong but because it was the Government's. 1815. If England withdrew from the Coalition, all resistance to Napoleon was at an end, for without England's subsidies the remaining powers could not keep their armies in the field, and the Emperor might resume his sway in Europe as early as he pleased. It was in this light that the coming campaign presented itself to Wellington. Now, more even than in the worst days of the Peninsular War, the existing Ministry depended upon him whether it should stand or fall; and upon the maintenance of the Ministry depended the defeat of Napoleon. A short semblance of success on the part of the enemy might suffice to bring about the great disaster. It may seem almost incredible that a few factious utterances by a handful of mediocre men—utterances inspired rather by vanity, by the habit of contention and the excitement of rhetorical combat than by any sincere desire to do mischief—should cramp the movements and vitiate the dispositions of a great commander in the field ; but undoubtedly they did so in 1815 ; and the consequences were likely to have been the more serious because the commander was, as he truly said, at the head of an infamous army.

# CHAPTER II

As a matter of fact Napoleon could have invaded Belgium with every chance of success at the end of March. Kleist and the Prince of Orange could not have raised, between them, more than eighty thousand men, of which number twenty-four thousand Saxons and Netherlanders were not to be trusted, and the remainder were mostly half-trained troops. Against them Napoleon could have pitted fifty thousand seasoned soldiers, and, encountering such commanders, could hardly have failed of a great initial success. The Prince and Kleist were prepared for such a movement, but could not agree where to meet it. The Prince of Orange, in his anxiety to take the offensive, had disposed his troops upon a line running from Tournai through Ath and along the course of the Sambre to Namur, where was stationed the Prussian vanguard ; and he was anxious to give battle on the south side of Brussels. Kleist, on the other hand, fearing for his communications, held the maintenance of the line of the Meuse to be the most important object. As a matter of strategic principle Sir Hudson Lowe agreed with Kleist, but considered that strategic considerations were overruled by the political inexpediency of throwing the entire country south of Brussels, already not too well affected towards the new King of the Netherlands, into the arms of Napoleon. Kleist and the Prince accordingly compromised their difference by arranging that, in case of an attack, the Prince's own army should retire while Kleist's should

advance, and that their united forces should give battle
at Tirlemont, about thirteen miles east of Brussels.
Wellington, as may be supposed, settled the
question immediately after his arrival by advocating
that the Prussian army and his own should unite at
once south of Brussels, rather than allow the French
to be in possession of the Belgian capital even for a
moment. The question was no easy one of solution.
The Prussian communications lay towards the east,
the British towards the west, the Dutch towards the
north. Which of them was to sacrifice its line of
operations in case of mishap ? Without immediately
raising this issue, Gneisenau consented to move
Prussian troops farther westward so that the most
advanced of them should occupy Charleroi and the
ground west of it so far as the Roman road from
Binche to Bavai, but asked for further light upon
Wellington's plans. The Duke in reply admitted
that political considerations counted for much in the
disposition which he advocated, and conceded further
that to allow them too much weight, as compared with
purely military exigencies, was as great a blunder as
the converse. He then gave it as his opinion that,
if Napoleon should advance, he would probably choose
the line between the Scheldt and the Sambre, or in
other words that he would strike at the British communications. In that case the Prussians at Charleroi
would form the left of the line, the rest of the
Prussians being concentrated at Namur. Battle would
then be offered south of Brussels, and, in case of
mishap, the entire army would retreat upon Liége
and Maastricht or even, if necessary, still farther east
to Juliers. This signified plainly that, if circumstances should demand it, the British and Dutch would
abandon their communications and shift their line of
operation eastward. Gneisenau, emphasising this
point, declared that all difficulties were now at an
end, and that he accepted Wellington's plan without hesitation. Wellington rejoined that only the

1815.
April-
May.

peculiarity of the circumstances could warrant him in thus giving up his connection with the sea ; but that any retreat of the Allies could at worst be but momentary—indeed they were already in too great strength to think of retreat or even of being attacked.[1]

This last opinion, written on the 13th of April, referred of course only to the situation of the moment and signified no more than that a raid from Napoleon with a small force, for the sake of rallying the Belgians to his standard, was now out of the question. On the other hand the collapse of the Duke of Angoulême's operations forbade an early offensive of the Allies such as Wellington had hoped to undertake in support of the royalists in France. The British Commander now turned his attention rather to the defence of the Low Countries, hastening the repair of the fortresses in West Flanders within the quadrilateral Ostend, Ypres, Mons, Antwerp, and offering to supply twelve thousand of the twenty-seven thousand men required for their garrisons from his British and Hanoverian infantry. On the 21st of April Blücher arrived at Liége, upon which point the Prussian army was rapidly assembling ; and Wellington, bidding him welcome, sent Colonel Henry Hardinge as British attaché to the Prussian head-quarters.

Throughout this time an infinity of business was pressed upon Wellington. There were long letters as to the attitude of Spain, equally long letters as to the prospects of obtaining a contingent from Portugal, constant references to the business transacted, or untransacted, at Vienna, the soreness of Prussia at being restrained from swallowing up Saxony, the allotment of the German contingents to the armies of Blücher and of the Duke himself, the arrangements for the subsistence, upon Netherlandish territory, of the Prussian armies, which as usual were extremely arbitrary and rapacious, above all the distribution of

[1] *Wellington Desp.* To Gneisenau, 5th, 10th, 15th April; to Clancarty, 6th April 1815. *Supp. Desp.* x. 45, 69.

the subsidies to hungry and impecunious powers, 1815.
whose representatives vied with each other in April-
parading the sacrifices and poverty of their nations. May.
Everything was thrown upon him ; and, as holder
in some degree of the English purse-strings, he was
treated by his German colleagues of all professions,
Blücher perhaps excepted, with a kind of jealous
servility. It was no easy course that was given him
to steer ; and indeed his functions during this campaign, as in the Peninsula, were perhaps even more
diplomatic than military.

In the matter of his relations with the Prussians
there were two initial difficulties. First, the Prussian
army was divided into rival parties, headed by Generals
Knesebeck and Gneisenau ; and, since Knesebeck for
his own ends favoured close joint action between the
British and Prussians, it was natural that Gneisenau
should cherish a contrary view. In the second place,
Wellington's feelings towards France were widely
different from the Prussian. Gneisenau not unnaturally, considering all that his adopted country had
suffered at the hands of the French armies, was for
making the war one of punishment for the French
nation, and a means of "humbling their military spirit."
Wellington wished only to get rid of Napoleon, and to
spare the French as much as possible. It was thus
that he had rendered the approach of the red-coats
more welcome than that of Soult's soldiers to the inhabitants of Southern France. Some substitute for
Napoleon must, however, be found, and Wellington
agreed with Castlereagh in thinking that the restoration
of Lewis the Eighteenth would be the most certain
means of assuring the tranquillity of Europe for a
short time. But all reports from France were so
unfavourable to this solution, and the Tsar Alexander
was known to be so adverse to it, that Wellington,
while still working for it, thought success almost impossible of attainment.[1]

[1] *Wellington Supp. Desp.* x. 79, 138, 173.

1815.    All through April British reinforcements continued
May. slowly to trickle over to Flanders, and at the end of
the month Lord Uxbridge arrived to take command
May 1. of the cavalry.   On the 1st of May there was an
alarm of an attack, and Wellington issued alternative
orders for a concentration of the British and Netherlandish armies to meet a French advance either
between the Lys and the Scheldt or between the Scheldt
and the Sambre.   In the first case the inundations
about Oudenarde and Ghent were to be let loose ;
and the British were to concentrate between the Scheldt
and the Sambre in readiness to cross the former river,
while the Netherlanders were to assemble at Soignies
and Nivelles.   In the second event both British and
Netherlanders were to be gathered together at Enghien
and Soignies.   The intent was very evidently to cover
Ghent and Brussels, the temporary home of King
Lewis and the newly established capital of King
May 3. William.   On the 3rd of May Wellington rode over
to Tirlemont to meet Blücher, with whom he had a
conversation which he described as very satisfactory,
the purport of it being, apparently, that Blücher had
promised to stand by him and not allow him to be
overwhelmed by superior numbers.   Since the armies
of the two Marshals combined amounted to one hundred and fifty thousand men, and Napoleon's, by all
reports, did not exceed one hundred and fifteen thousand, Wellington had hopes of " giving a good
account even of Bonaparte." [1]

The alarm passed off, and the next incident was
a mutiny of Blücher's fourteen thousand Saxon troops,
which compelled their removal from the fighting line
to the rear.   This was no very great matter, for the
loyalty of these Saxons had always been doubtful,
and it was better that they should declare themselves
at a safe moment than in the middle of active operations ;  but it is significant that the King of Saxony

[1] *Wellington Desp.* Memo. from the Prince of Orange, 1st
May. To Prince of Orange and Hardenberg, 3rd May 1815.

entreated Wellington to take them under his command,[1] 1815.
attributing their misconduct entirely to rude handling May.
on the part of the Prussians, and engaging to answer
for their fidelity if subjected to the Duke.   In the
course of the month the English battalions promised
to Wellington commenced to cross the Channel in
driblets, and he began to chafe at the delay in opening
the campaign.   He had fairly good intelligence of
the strength of the enemy from Clarke, Napoleon's
late Minister of War, who was now with Lewis the
Eighteenth at Ghent ;  and he was satisfied that the
British and Prussians could not move until the main
body of the Allies should come up ;  but none the less
he had an uneasy feeling that every day gained by
Napoleon was to the advantage of the enemy.   Intelligence from the frontier continued to be contradictory.
On the 8th of May the Duke wrote that he and May 8.
Blücher were so well united and so strong that he had
little apprehension of an attack.   On the 9th, upon May 9.
the news of a French concentration at Valenciennes
and Maubeuge, he was inclined to contract his cantonments a little.   A few days later there were signs
that the enemy contemplated a defensive rather than
an offensive campaign ;  but, in accordance with concerted arrangements, the Prussians drew a little closer
to the British, and on the 11th of May Blücher fixed May 11.
his head-quarters at Hannut, about twenty miles west
of Liége.   Still the prevailing impression both at the
British and the Prussian head-quarters was that their
armies were doomed to a tedious series of sieges of
the French fortresses on the frontier ; and Gneisenau
was inclined to think that the operations would require
five hundred siege-cannon.[2]   On the 22nd of May May 22.
French patrols encountered the Prince of Orange's
outposts, a little to the east and to the south of Mons,
and fired the first shots of the campaign ;  but the
incident was of no importance.   On the 21st Wellington announced that, though still without some of the

---

[1] *Supp. Desp.* x. 346, 348.          [2] *Ibid.* x. 335.

1815. German contingents that had been promised to him,
May. he could, after making provision for all garrisons,
take the field with seventy-six thousand bayonets and
May 30. sabres ;[1] and on the 30th he wrote to Uxbridge that
there was a prospect of moving shortly.[2] Blücher was
impatient to open the campaign ; and it was hoped
that, upon the arrival of the Austrians on the Rhine
at about the middle of June, the entire force under the
Prince and Wellington would advance in earnest.[3]

June. In the first days of June there were again reports
of a French concentration at Maubeuge, and Wellington on the 7th issued his final orders as to the defence
of the fortresses of Western Flanders.[4] French news-
papers, carefully falsified, announced that Napoleon
would leave Paris for Laon on the 6th. Another
report[5] said that he would go to Douai on the same
day, would make a false attack on the Prussians and
a real attack on the English, and destroy both before
the Russians came up. The air was full of rumours
and contradictions ; and Napoleon was reported to be
at half a dozen different places before he had ever left
June 10. Paris. On the 10th Clarke sent a final estimate of
the strength and distribution of the French force,
reckoning the troops at Napoleon's disposal in the
north very correctly at one hundred and twenty
June 11. thousand men. On the 11th a Colonel Dillon of the
British army arrived at Mons, and gave it as certain
intelligence that Napoleon had reached Avesnes. On
June 12. the 12th five deserters came into Mons from Landrecies
with information that Napoleon was just come to
Laon. Other intelligencers brought news that Reille's
corps had reached Maubeuge ; that a division of
the Imperial Guard was due to arrive at Avesnes,
to which place head-quarters would be transferred

---

[1] *Wellington Desp.* To Schwartzenberg, 21st May 1815.
[2] *Ibid.* To Uxbridge, 1st June 1815.
[3] *Ibid.* To H. Wellesley, 2nd June 1815.
[4] *Ibid.* To Prince of Orange, 7th June 1815. *Supp. Desp.* x.
412, 413.
[5] *Supp. Desp.* x. 424.

immediately, and that Soult had passed through Valen- 1815.
ciennes and Maubeuge, *incognito*, also on his way to
Avesnes.[1]    On the 13th there were reports from more June 13.
than one source of a French concentration at Maubeuge ; and on the 14th the troops at Maubeuge were June 14.
stated to be moving eastward upon Beaumont.    Early
in the afternoon General Dörnberg wrote to head-
quarters that, according to the latest accounts, there
were one hundred thousand men between Maubeuge
and Philippeville ; and Hardinge at ten o'clock of
the same night announced that at the Prussian head-
quarters a French attack was expected, and that some
preliminary orders had been given tending towards
the concentration of the Prussian army to meet it.
Nevertheless the Allied armies both of Wellington
and Blücher remained in their original cantonments,
which, as shall now be shown, were of dangerous
extension.

On the right or west of the line the head-quarters
of Hill's, the Second Corps, were at Ath.    Of his two
British divisions, Colville's head-quarters were at
Oudenarde ; the division being thrown back more or
less *en potence*, with one of its Hanoverian brigades at
Nieuport, Mitchell's brigade about Renaix, and Johnstone's between Courtrai and Oudenarde.    Clinton's
head-quarters were at Ath, where was stationed Du
Plat's brigade of the German Legion ; the Fifty-second
and a Hanoverian brigade being posted between the
town and Lessines, with the remainder of Adam's
brigade at Leuze.    Next to these, east of Colville and
north of Clinton, were Stedman's Netherlandish division, with head-quarters at Sotteghem, cantonments
scattered between that village and Ghent, and Anthing's
Dutch brigade still farther north at Alost.

The First Army Corps, under the Prince of Orange,
had its head-quarters at Braine-le-Comte.    Of Cooke's
British division the Guards were at Enghien and Byng's
brigade at the village of Marcq, practically touching

---

[1] *Supp. Desp.* x. 456.

1815.
June 14. the Guards.  The head-quarters of Alten's division were at Soignies ; Colin Halkett's brigade had been distributed south-westward of it as far as Lens, Kielmansegge's Hanoverians a little to south of Halkett, and Ompteda's north-westward towards Ath.  Farther east, Chassé's Netherlandish division, with headquarters at Roeulx, was disposed southward towards Binche, and Perponcher's, with head-quarters at Nivelles, reached as far south-eastward as Frasnes and Villers Perwin.  The Reserve was assembled in and about Brussels.

The British and Hanoverian cavalry were distributed along the line of the Haine from Mons by Jemappes, St. Ghislain, Roucourt and Béclers to Tournai and Menin, with two regiments at Ghent, and a brigade between Ninove and Grammont, at which last place were Uxbridge's head-quarters.  General Dörnberg, who commanded the 3rd Brigade, was stationed at Mons and charged with the collection of intelligence from the frontier.  Eastward from Mons the Netherlandish cavalry watched the frontier as far as Binche, from which point, or rather from Bonne Esperance, a little farther south, they were relieved by the Prussians.

The Ist Prussian Corps, under Ziethen, had its head-quarters at Charleroi and extended from Fontaine l'Évêque on the west through Marchienne to Moustier on the east, its reserves of infantry being at Fleurus, of cavalry at Sombreffe, and of artillery at Gembloux.  Its outposts ran from Bonne Esperance, south-eastward through Thuin and Gerpinnes to Sosoye, a total front of close on thirty miles.

On Ziethen's left the IInd Corps, under General von Pirch I.,[1] had its head-quarters and one brigade at Namur, another parallel to it on the Meuse at Huy, a third midway between them to the north at Heron, the fourth at Thorombais-les-Béguignes, eighteen miles

---

[1] There was a second General von Pirch in command of a brigade of Ziethen's corps, who is distinguished as Pirch II.

due north of Namur, the reserve infantry on the road between these two places, and the reserve artillery at Hannut.

The IIIrd Corps had its head-quarters and one brigade at Ciney, about fifteen miles south-east of Namur ; the reserve artillery lay on the road to Namur, with a second brigade of foot north-west of it at Assesse, and the reserve cavalry on the road to Dinant, where there was a third brigade of infantry. The fourth brigade of infantry lay at Huy.

Of the IVth Corps one brigade was with head-quarters at Liége; another a little to the north at Liers, with the reserve cavalry and artillery a short distance to north-east of it ; a third brigade lay five miles to west of Liége at Hollogne-aux-Pierres, and the fourth still farther to west at Waremme.

The shape of the line thus held from Ostend through Tournai and Mons to Liége was convex, and in its full extent about one hundred and fifty miles, of which, roughly speaking, one hundred miles were guarded by the hundred and five thousand men under Wellington and fifty by the hundred and twenty thousand men of Blücher. The head-quarters of the two chiefs, Brussels and Namur, were thirty-two miles apart by road. Taking Nivelles, immediately to north of Fontaine l'Evêque, as the point of junction between the two armies, the remotest of the Prussians at Liége and of the British at Oudenarde could not possibly have reached it in less than two days. This dispersion was explained by Wellington, so far as his army was concerned, by the imperative necessity for watching the four great roads that led from Lille, Condé, and Valenciennes upon Ghent and Brussels. It was on one or other of these lines, it must be repeated, that he looked for an attack, if any should be delivered. He had therefore arranged his dispositions to concentrate either to west or to south ; he had made fortified passages over the rivers ; and he had repaired the fortresses of Nieuport, Ostend, Ypres, Menin, Cour-

1815.
June 14.

trai, Oudenarde, Tournai, Ath and Mons, so as to place the weakest of them beyond reach of a stroke of surprise, and to make the strongest of them defy any onslaught less formidable than a regular siege. A hostile concentration at Maubeuge in itself by no means belied his prevision, for the enemy might advance from thence as readily upon Mons as upon Charleroi or any other point upon the Sambre. Assuming then that he had rightly divined his enemy's purpose, which the event showed that he had not, his arrangements were intelligible.

The like can hardly be said of the Prussians. The dissemination of their army was excused upon the ground that, if the cantonments were contracted, the victualling of the force became impossible. There was no doubt some truth in this ; though it seems that the difficulty was greatly of the Prussian's own making, for they deliberately imported dissension into the ranks of the Allies by endeavouring to take their subsistence by force from the Netherlanders instead of paying for it.[1]  But in any case the disposition of the IIIrd Corps within the triangle between Namur, Huy and Dinant, facing west, seems to be absolutely meaningless as a defensive measure ; and, as Wellington pointed out, pending the arrival of the Austrians and Russians, the attitude of the Allied armies in the Low Countries was inevitably defensive. If any French offensive movement were apprehended from Philippeville, a small corps of cavalry would have sufficed to watch Dinant and the line of the Meuse southward from Namur. If again Gneisenau dreaded a blow at his communications, after the manner of Saxe and Carnot, the obvious precaution was to shift his line of operations from Liége and Namur to the great Roman road, which runs through Tongres to Maastricht, and to have moved the IIIrd and IVth Corps farther to

[1] This gave Wellington much trouble. See *Despatches*. To Clancarty, 14th May ; to Hardinge, 24th May 1815. *Supp. Desp.* x. 368, 380.

the north.   But he, even as Wellington, thought his 1815.
own army too strong to be attacked; and the June 14.
arrangements of both were made rather for the coming
invasion of France than for the defence of the Low
Countries.

Still more curious were Gneisenau's orders and
measures in case of an attack on the line of the Sambre.
There were bridges at Lobbes, Thuin, Abbaye d'Aulne,
Marchienne, Charleroi and Châtelet, all of which lay
within the sphere of observation of Ziethen's corps.
No attempt was made to prepare these for demolition;
indeed the bare fact that they were of masonry was
accepted in the Prussian army as warrant that they
were indestructible.   Further, orders were issued by
Gneisenau that no gun was to be unlimbered on the
bridges, and that their defence was to be limited to
a powerful fire of skirmishers.   At this rate it is
difficult to understand why the Prussian General went
through the form of stationing three brigades of
infantry on the river at all ;  for a few vedettes might
perfectly well have watched the points of passage if
there were no intention to defend them.   But it is fairly
evident that Gneisenau still cherished a predilection
for the cordon-system which had ruined the Austrian
campaign of the Low Countries in 1793 and 1794.
However, Ziethen's instructions were, in case he were
assailed in force, to abandon the whole of the ground
that he had been watching from Bonne Esperance to
Châtelet and to concentrate at Fleurus ; which meant
that he was to retire to a flank, leaving a gap of over
fifteen miles in the Allied line from Binche to beyond
Charleroi, and uncovering the direct road from
Charleroi to Brussels by Quatre-Bras.   One wonders
whether this was part of the " satisfactory " arrangement agreed to between Blücher and Wellington.
The Duke had freely offered, in case of a reverse, to
abandon his line of communication with the sea and
to retreat eastward; and upon this understanding
Gneisenau had consented to bring his army forward

1815. and help Wellington to keep the enemy, if possible,
June 14. out of Belgium.    But, if at the first serious thrust at
its line of outposts the Prussian advanced corps were
to shrink away to eastward and throw open the direct
road to Brussels, then obviously Wellington must
either conform to the movement, making a flank march
across the front of the assailing army, or retire northward, if not westward, and be wholly separated from
Blücher.    The neglect of this important point seems
to reflect no great credit upon the foresight of either
commander.

Such was the situation when cumulative intelligence
of the assembly of the French about Maubeuge, Beaumont and Philippeville caused Gneisenau at noon of
the 14th to order Thielmann and Bülow to contract the
cantonments of the Prussian IIIrd and IVth Corps.
Further information received later in the day prompted
him,[1] shortly before midnight, to send further and more
definite instructions with a view to the concentration
of the entire army.    Thielmann was to leave small
detachments to watch Dinant and the approaches to
Givet, and bring the rest of his force to the left bank
of the Meuse about Namur ; Pirch I. was to collect
the IInd Corps between Namur and Fleurus at Mazy
and Onoz ; and Bülow was politely requested to
gather the IVth Corps about Hannut on the 15th and
to fix his head-quarters there.    But no hint was given
to Bülow that this movement was to be part of a
general concentration ; and not a word was sent to
Wellington to inform him that such a concentration
had even been thought of.

Meanwhile Napoleon had been laying his plans
with his best skill.    He had early resolved to take
the offensive, and to assail the Allies in Flanders,
hoping that, by beating Blücher's and Wellington's
armies in turn, he would rally all Belgium to his
standard, bring a peace-loving ministry into power at
Downing Street, and be free to march with his

---

[1] Blücher was asleep, so Gneisenau took the duty upon himself

victorious army to the Vosges to throw back the 1815.
Austrians and Prussians.  It was open to him to June.
strike at the Allies by their right flank, their left
flank, or their centre.   He rejected the first and second
plans because, in addition to incidental objections, the
turning of either flank would drive the British to unite
with the Prussians, or the Prussians to unite with the
British, whereas his purpose was to keep them apart and
if possible to defeat them piecemeal.   He considered
that nothing less than a victory would drive the British
Ministers from power, whereas Wellington, who was
the better judge on such a point, conceived that the
occupation of even half of Belgium would suffice;
and therein lies the root of the difference of opinion
between them, which reacted so powerfully upon the
conduct of the campaign.   Napoleon therefore decided
to fall upon the armies of Blücher and Wellington at
their point of junction with all possible secrecy and
swiftness.

At the beginning of June the five corps of the
Army of the North were posted about Lille, Valenciennes, Mezières, Thionville and Soissons, with the
Imperial Guard at Paris, and the Reserve Cavalry
between the Aisne and the Sambre.   Screened by the
fortresses on the frontier and by the belt of forest that
extends from Thuin almost to Namur on the south of
the Sambre, the concentration of these forces was to
such a master of the art no difficult matter, and was
rendered the easier by the unwillingness of the Allies
to send even the smallest military bodies across the
frontier.   The Imperial Guard were the first to move,
marching in detachments between the 5th and the June 5-8.
8th of June upon Avesnes by way of Soissons ; Gérard
with the 4th Corps was the next, leaving Metz on
the 6th for Philippeville; d'Erlon quitted Lille on the
9th for Valenciennes, from which Reille moved out at
his approach, and the two marched eastward upon
Maubeuge.  Vandamme shifted from Mezières to
Philippeville, and the rest of the troops were directed

1815. to Beaumont.   Napoleon himself left Paris early on
June 12. the 12th, breakfasted at Soissons, slept at Laon, and
arrived at Avesnes on the 13th.   By the night of the
June 14. 14th the whole were assembled on a line of about
sixteen miles between Solre-sur-Sambre and Philippeville.   The entire manœuvre was conducted with the
strictest secrecy ;   all communication with Belgium
and the Rhine provinces was closed ;   an embargo was
laid on all ships even to the very fishing-boats ;   and
at every point from which regular troops had been
withdrawn, National Guards were pushed up to take
their place.   Only one small detail went amiss.   Soult
omitted to send the requisite orders to Grouchy for the
march of the cavalry, and it was only upon Napoleon's
arrival at Laon, where were Grouchy's head-quarters,
that the mistake was corrected.   Even so the whole of
the horse arrived at Avesnes on the night of the 13th,
though not without forced marches exhausting to both
beasts and men.

Thus the information which had reached the Allied
commanders on the 12th, 13th and 14th was in the
main correct.   The movements of the Guard, of
d'Erlon and Reille were accurately given, and the
progress of Soult, *incognito*, was truly reported.   It
must, however, be said for Wellington and Blücher
that marches and counter-marches of French troops
upon the northern frontier had for weeks been incessant, and that, until the very end, any attempt to
piece them together as an indication of the enemy's
plans was hopeless.   Both of the Allied Commanders
have been reproached for not making greater use of
their cavalry to penetrate Napoleon's intentions ;   but
it seems to be literally true that both of them, and not
Wellington only, were embarrassed by uncertainty
whether they were at war or at peace.   Bülow pleaded
his ignorance of the fact, that there had been no declaration of war, in excuse for the slowness of his movements,
shortly to be narrated, on the 15th of June.   Napoleon
himself on the 7th of June denounced the action of

England in capturing a French frigate in the Medi- 1815.
terranean, as "bloodshed during peace"; and, as if June 14.
conscious that the signal for opening the war lay
with himself, he wrote definitely to Davoût on the 11th
of June that hostilities would begin on the 14th.
This peculiarity of the situation has, as it seems to
me, escaped the notice of most of the later writers
upon the campaign of 1815. It is urged by at least
one of them that the manifesto of the Allied Powers
of the 13th of March was in itself a declaration of war;
but it was rather a decree of outlawry against an
individual whose authority as ruler of France was
expressly set aside. The document certainly implied
that those who followed Napoleon's banner would do
so at their peril; but beyond question, if the Allies
had invaded France before Napoleon attacked them,
they would have issued a proclamation calling upon
all Frenchmen to dissociate themselves from him and
promising them good treatment if they should do so.
The Powers of Europe were dealing, as they well knew,
with a military revolt, not with a national movement;
and it would have been impolitic as well as contrary
to their professions to treat the French nation as if it
were the French army. On the other hand, it may
justly be argued that, given such a state of uncertainty
and the presence of a French host under Napoleon,
the utmost care should have been taken that everything
should be ready against a sudden attack. On the
contrary, both Blücher and Wellington were so confident of their superiority that they took less instead
of more than the ordinary precautions, feeling sure
that Napoleon would not venture upon an offensive
movement. They were wrong in their divination of
his intentions; but their trust in their own strength
was justified by the result.[1]

On the 14th, the anniversary of Marengo and
Friedland, Napoleon issued the last of those stirring

---

[1] *Corres. de Napoléon*, 22023, 22040. Pollio, *Waterloo* (French
translation), 101, 129 *n.*

appeals which had so often stimulated his armies to victory, and in the evening dictated his justly famous orders for the movements of the morrow.    The army was to advance upon Charleroi in three principal columns; Reille's and d'Erlon's corps on the left by Thuin and Marchienne ; Vandamme's and Lobau's corps, the Imperial Guard and Grouchy's reserve of cavalry in the centre by Ham-sur-Heure and Marcinelle ; Gérard's corps by Florennes and Gerpinnes.    The whole were to be covered by a screen of cavalry from the centre column and headed by Domont's three regiments of mounted chasseurs, with Pajol's corps of six more regiments of light horse and two battalions of horse-artillery in support.    Domont was to start at half-past two in the morning, Pajol and the heads of the infantry at three o'clock ;  the foot taking the main roads and the horse the by-roads.    Reille, Vandamme, Pajol and Gérard were to keep themselves in constant communication with each other so as to arrive in one united mass before Charleroi.    In the centre column the 3rd Corps was to take the lead, to be followed by the 6th Corps at four o'clock and by the various sections of the Guard at half-hourly intervals between five and six.    The pontoon-train was to provide three sections to throw as many bridges over the Sambre, which the Emperor intended to cross with his whole army before noon, he himself accompanying the advanced guard of the centre column.    For the general purposes of the campaign he designed to divide his army into two wings and a reserve, the left wing under Ney, who was on the point of joining him, the right under Grouchy, and the reserve, which would be strengthened from one wing or the other, according to circumstances, under his personal command.

At half-past three in the morning of the 15th the French vanguards crossed the Netherlandish frontier at Leers, Cour-sur-Heure and Thy-le-Chateau ; but whether from neglect on the part of the staff or indolence on the part of the generals, there was delay in the

march of the rear of the columns.   D'Erlon did not
set the 1st Corps in motion until half-past four, instead
of at three, as he had been bidden.   The officer who
was carrying the orders to Vandamme was disabled
through a fall from his horse ; and, as Soult sent no
second messenger, Vandamme had no knowledge of
the intended movement until Lobau's corps came up
to his bivouac.   The 4th Corps, which should have
marched from Philippeville at three, did not reach
Florennes—a distance of not more than five miles—
until seven o'clock, and was there bewildered and
dismayed by the desertion to the Allies of one of its
divisional generals, Bourmont, together with the whole
of his staff.   However, the advanced parties on the
French centre and left in due time came into collision
with the outposts of Pirch I.'s brigade, and pressed
them slowly back from position to position until
between nine and ten o'clock they reached the Sambre
at Marchienne and Charleroi, and found the bridges
barricaded and defended by infantry and guns.
General Bachelu, whose division led Reille's column,
threw away two hours before he finally cleared the
passage at Marchienne.   Even then, the bridge being
narrow, it took four hours for Reille's corps to defile
over the river ; and d'Erlon's corps in consequence
did not even begin to cross until half-past four.   Pajol
having failed to carry the bridge of Charleroi by a
charge of hussars, waited till eleven o'clock for the
arrival of Vandamme's infantry, which, having started
late, was still far away ; when up came Napoleon
himself with a portion of the Young Guard, which, on
learning of Vandamme's mishap, he had brought
forward by cross-roads.   Under the Emperor's direction, the barricade was soon broken down ;  the
Prussians retired, and Pajol detaching one regiment
—the 1st Hussars—due north towards Gosselies and
Quatre-Bras to clear the front of the left column, led
his main body north-east upon Fleurus on the track
of the retreating Prussians.

1815.    Waiting at Charleroi to watch his troops defile
June 15. over the river, Napoleon received at about two o'clock
a message that the Prussians were showing themselves
in force in Gosselies, and directed Reille to march
his corps in that direction, sending meanwhile the light
cavalry of the Guard under Lefebvre-Desnoëttes to support the 1st Hussars. D'Erlon was presently instructed to follow Reille, and Ney, reporting himself
to the Emperor at three o'clock, was bidden to take
command of this, the left wing, proceed to Gosselies
and advance along the road to Brussels. At half-past
three orders were sent to Gérard to make for the
bridge at Châtelet instead of that at Charleroi, as
originally ordered ; and meanwhile, as Vandamme's
and Grouchy's troops debouched from the bridge, they
were pushed north-eastward along the road to Gilly.

To deal first with the left wing, Reille's advanced
cavalry was checked at Jumet by some of Ziethen's
light horse and sharp-shooters, who were covering the
retirement of Steinmetz's brigade from Fontaine
l'Évêque through Gosselies upon Fleurus. After
some delay the mounted troops on both sides came
into collision ; but there was no decisive result until
the French infantry, which had been hurried forward
by Reille, came up, drove the sharp-shooters from
Gosselies and occupied the village. Steinmetz's main
body at this moment was still to west of Gosselies and
therefore cut off from the direct road to Fleurus ;
but with great decision he launched such troops as he
had at hand upon the French as they issued from the
village, drove them back and, by holding in force the
houses at the north end, was able to draw off the bulk
of his brigade north-eastward to Heppignies and so
to its appointed destination. However, the road to
Brussels was now thrown open ; and Ney, who had
come up in the course of the combat, pushed Lefebvre-
Desnoëttes's cavalry northward upon Quatre-Bras and
directed Bachelu's infantry to follow him for three
miles, as far as Mellet, in support.

Lefebvre-Desnoëttes met with no resistance until he 1815. reached Frasnes, about five miles north of Gosselies, June 15. where he came upon a battalion and a battery of Prince Bernhard of Saxe-Weimar's Nassau brigade, which lay in and about Quatre-Bras. The village had been prepared for defence ; and, as the Nassauers showed a resolute front, Lefebvre sent a party round the eastern flank of his opponents, who thereupon retired to the border of the wood of Bossu, about a mile and a half to the south of Quatre-Bras. Following them up, Lefebvre found himself stopped abruptly by superior forces at this point ; for Prince Bernhard of Saxe-Weimar, anticipating the orders of his divisional commander, Perponcher, had concentrated his brigade at Quatre-Bras and had sent two more battalions and a battery to reinforce his advanced party. Having only cavalry, and those of inferior numbers, under his hand, Lefebvre realised that it was impossible for him to attack. It was now nearly seven o'clock ; and, even if he were to summon infantry from Gosselies, they could hardly come up before dark. He therefore fell back for the night to Frasnes, where a battalion of infantry joined him soon after sunset. He then sent in his report to Ney, giving the important information, gleaned from prisoners, that the troops which he had encountered at Frasnes had nothing to do with those that had been engaged at Gosselies. The latter, he explained, had retired eastward upon Fleurus ; the former were under Wellington's command ; and the bulk of the Netherlandish army lay westward about Mons with head-quarters at Braine-le-Comte.[1]

In the centre Pirch II. had occupied a strong position in rear of Gilly, with his front covered by a boggy rivulet ; his seven battalions being skilfully disposed to present a great appearance of strength, and his flank towards the Sambre being watched by a regiment of dragoons. Grouchy, who had galloped

[1] A translation of the full text of this letter is printed by Col. James, p. 74.

forward to reconnoitre, would not venture to attack without orders ; whereupon Napoleon hurried to the spot and, taking in the situation at a glance, directed him to assail Pirch II.'s front with one of Vandamme's divisions, to turn his left flank with Exelmans's corps of cavalry and to push on to Sombreffe.   This done —the time being about half-past three—the Emperor returned to Charleroi to hasten the march of Vandamme's infantry ; but, hearing no sound of an engagement, he rode back soon after half-past five to Gilly and ordered Vandamme and Grouchy to attack immediately.   Pirch II. thereupon began to retire, and, though some of his battalions were caught and very severely handled by the French cavalry, he made good his retreat with some loss to Fleurus, and was there allowed to rest in peace.   Pajol's and Exelmans's troopers then bivouacked to south of Fleurus, covering Vandamme's infantry ;  and  Vandamme and Pajol sent in their reports to the Emperor.   Vandamme's was to the effect that the Prussians, whom he reckoned at ten to fifteen thousand men, were in full retreat, having left only outposts of cavalry in Fleurus ; and Pajol confirmed this by stating that, if Vandamme had given him some infantry, he could have taken Fleurus. Their testimony therefore avouched the fact that the Allies had withdrawn towards the north-east.

On the right, Gérard's corps, having marched upon Charleroi, was delayed rather than hastened by the order that changed its direction to Châtelet, and hence only one of his divisions had crossed the Sambre before dark.

At nightfall therefore the French were thus posted according to Napoleon's distribution into two wings and a reserve.   Of the right wing Pajol's and Exelmans's cavalry lay between Lambusart and Campinaire ; Vandamme's corps in and to the east of Soleilmont forest ; Hulot's division of Gérard's corps at Châtelineau, and the three remaining divisions south of the Sambre at Châtelet.   Of the left wing the light

cavalry of the Guard was at Frasnes.  Reille's corps 1815.
was banked up in rear of it on the road to Brussels. June 15.
D'Erlon's corps was at Marchienne, Bachelu's division
lying at Mellet, Foy's and Jerome's in and about
Gosselies, and Girard's division a little further to the
east at Wangenies.  Of the Reserve, the Young Guard
was at Gilly, the Old Guard between that village and
Charleroi, and the whole of Lobau's corps on the south
bank of the Sambre.  On the whole, therefore,
Napoleon's first day's work had prospered.  He had
not reached the road which was the line of junction
between the inner flanks of the Allies—the road, that
is to say, which runs south-eastward from Nivelles to
Namur—nor had he thrown more than two-thirds of
his army across the Sambre ;  but he had struck the
advanced guards of both of the Allied armies and had
found no main body massed behind them.  He had
met with brave but not very strenuous resistance; he
had inflicted substantial loss—some twelve hundred
killed, wounded and prisoners—upon Ziethen's corps;
and the two Allied armies had retired by divergent
routes, the Netherlanders to the north and the Prussians
to the east.  So far, then, all seemed to promise well
for his plan of forcing those two armies apart and
beating each of them independently of the other.

On the side of the Allies the fact of the French
advance became known to General Ziethen at half-
past four in the morning of the 15th, through the
sound of Reille's cannon and musketry when he fell
upon Steinmetz's brigade at Thuin.  Ziethen at once
sent information to Blücher and fired the guns which
gave the signal of alarm.  At a quarter-past eight he
despatched a second message reporting that the French
had pushed back the Prussian advanced parties and
had crossed the Sambre in force, that Napoleon was
present in person with his Guard, and that the brigades
of Steinmetz and Pirch II. were falling back to
Gosselies and Gilly.  He added that he had sent this
intelligence to Wellington, with a request that the

1815.
June 15.

Duke should concentrate his army at Nivelles, in accordance with an intimation which General Müffling, Prussian attaché at the British head-quarters, had given on the previous day. To the first of these despatches Blücher replied that the IInd, IIIrd and IVth Corps had been ordered to concentrate, and that by evening they would be respectively at Onoz and Mazy, at Namur and at Hannut; and he added injunctions to observe the enemy closely, and to watch the old Roman road and in particular the neighbourhood of Binche. The substance of the second despatch was at once forwarded to Wellington's head-quarters by Gneisenau, with the further intelligence that the Prussian head-quarters would presently be transferred to Sombreffe, where they would await intelligence of Wellington's intentions. The whole of the Prussian army would likewise assemble on the morning of the 16th at Sombreffe, where Blücher intended to accept battle.

On Wellington's side of the field the Prince of Orange rode out at five in the morning to St. Symphorien, two miles east of Mons, whence, finding all quiet, he rode to Brussels to dine with Wellington. At noon there reached his head-quarters at Braine-le-Comte a letter from General Behr at Mons, reporting a French attack upon General Steinmetz and a lively fire about Charleroi, and adding that there was no sign of the enemy about Mons. This missive was at once forwarded by General Constant de Rebecque to Brussels, where the Prince of Orange communicated it to Wellington at three o'clock in the afternoon. A little later, further information came into Braine-le-Comte from General Chassé at Haine St. Pierre and General van Merlen at St. Symphorien, confirming the purport of Behr's letter, but containing the additional details that Steinmetz had evacuated Binche and would collect his brigade first at Gosselies. At two o'clock Constant forwarded this news also to Wellington ; and apparently at about the same time he sent orders to Perponcher to assemble his 1st brigade on the paved road near Nivelles, and his 2nd at Quatre-Bras, and to Generals Chassé and Collaert to gather their divisions together, the former at Fayt, the latter behind the Haine. Prince Bernhard of Saxe-Weimar had already placed his brigade in position at Quatre-Bras before receipt of any instruction from Perponcher ; but it does not appear that he sent in any report to Brussels of the approach of the French to his front.

The next intelligence, therefore, that Wellington received, so far as can be conjectured, was that despatched by Ziethen from Charleroi at nine in the morning, which arrived between three and four o'clock ; the rider having taken six hours to traverse thirty-four miles. An hour or so later Constant's second report came in. Müffling pressed Wellington to say whether he would concentrate his army, and where. The Duke answered that until he had further intelligence from Mons—for his latest report from that quarter was of half-past ten in the morning—he could not say, but that he would direct the whole army to be in readiness to march at any moment. This accordingly he did at six o'clock,[1] and at the same time he directed the Fourth Division on his extreme right to close in eastward from Oudenarde to Grammont. Further, the Prince of Orange was instructed to assemble the 2nd and 3rd Netherlandish divisions at Nivelles, and, if that place should have been attacked in course of the day, to summon thither also the First and Third British Divisions. At seven o'clock Müffling sent the purport of these orders to Gneisenau, adding that the Reserve, or a part of it, would move southward from Brussels when the moon rose. He also gave Wellington's judgment of the situation by the light of the very imperfect intelligence so far supplied to him. The

[1] The date 5 P.M. in *Wellington Desp.* is a mistake or a misprint. See James, p. 96, note.

enemy—such was the Duke's view—intended either to follow the Sambre downward in order to join other columns which were coming up from the direction of Givet, or to attack in the neighbourhood of Fleurus and, in all probability, in that of Nivelles at the same time. Wellington's object was to be in position to meet this latter onslaught. If it were not delivered, then he would bring the whole of his force to Nivelles on the morrow, ready to support the Prussians, or, if the Prussians should have been already assailed, to fall upon the enemy's flank and rear according to the arrangement already concerted with Blücher.

Some time later, probably near eight o'clock, came in Gneisenau's letter, which had been despatched from Namur soon after noon. Here again the bearer had failed in his duty, for he had taken from seven to eight hours to traverse forty miles. The contents of the letter did little to improve Wellington's knowledge. Gneisenau stated that Ziethen had orders not to retire beyond Fleurus if he could possibly help it ; and from this Wellington might infer that the bulk of the enemy's force had turned eastward ; but there was not a word to show that this was actually the case. There was not even a hint to indicate that Charleroi was in the enemy's hands. The news of the Prussian concentration at Sombreffe was really no news but simply a confirmation of an existing understanding. Once again, therefore, Wellington said that he must await intelligence from Mons before deciding upon the rendezvous for his army ; and it was not until ten o'clock that a letter came in from Dörnberg to say that there was nothing on his front. Thereupon Wellington sent out orders for the Reserve to march southward from Brussels to the cross-roads at Mont St. Jean, and for the rest of the army to make a general movement eastward, the Cavalry, Second and Fourth Divisions upon Enghien, the First Division upon Braine-le-Comte, and the Third Division upon Nivelles. This done, he went, together with most of his superior officers, to a ball given by the Duchess of Richmond in Brussels, hoping by his presence to discourage sanguine enemies and to hearten desponding friends.

Thus it was that when the hundred and twenty thousand men of Napoleon were bivouacked compactly within the quadrilateral Frasnes, Fleurus, Châtelet, Marchienne, Wellington's army was dispersed practically over the entire extent of its original cantonments, while Blücher's had hardly begun its concentration. It is idle to contend that the Allies were not, in the military sense, surprised ; but, masterly though was Napoleon's assembly of his troops, it was very greatly facilitated by the screen of fortresses and forest that lay ready to his hand, and far more than has been hitherto supposed by the fact that, so long as he remained within the boundaries of France, the Allies would not send even a patrol of cavalry to watch his movements. They could not have ventured to take the offensive and invade France without a declaration of their intentions, whereas it was open to Napoleon to cross the border and create a state of war whenever it might best suit him. " The enemy opened hostilities this morning," are the first words of Gneisenau's letter to Wellington ; and, though this had been in a manner expected, yet such temerity as Napoleon's in bearding a force of twice his strength was in itself something of a surprise. Nevertheless, the backwardness of Wellington's concentration was due in great measure to avoidable causes. The Prussians fought their " delaying actions " sturdily and well ; but their success shows that, if they had made better preparation for the defence and for the ultimate destruction of the bridges, they could have gained more time for the troops to assemble in their rear. More blameworthy by far was the omission of the Prussian staff to keep Wellington informed of the course of their proceedings during the day. It appears that Ziethen ceased to consider it his duty to report to the British Commander-in-Chief immediately after active operations had begun, that is to say, precisely at the moment when it was most necessary that Wellington should be fully apprised of all that was going forward. It was really monstrous that tidings of vital import should have been sent from Fleurus to Brussels by way of Namur, and that a journey of thirty miles should have been lengthened to nearly sixty. The tardiness of the despatch-riders was also disagreeably conspicuous ; and Wellington in after years commented with biting humour on the fact that the fattest man in the Prussian army had been selected to carry to him a message which should have been transmitted with all possible speed. It will be seen that these were not solitary examples of the inefficiency of the Prussian staff.

# CHAPTER III

AT the Duchess of Richmond's ball Wellington was
ostentatiously light of heart ; but towards one o'clock
on the morning of the 16th when the party had
sat down to supper, a third messenger came in
from Constant to the Prince of Orange with the news
that the French had advanced up to Quatre Bras.
Constant added that he had ordered Perponcher to
push forward his 1st brigade to the support of
Prince Bernhard's, and had warned Chassé and Collaert
to be prepared to march with the 3rd Netherlandish Division and the cavalry to the help of
Perponcher. It will be remembered that Wellington's orders of six o'clock had directed Perponcher's
and Chassé's divisions to assemble at Nivelles. These
orders came to Constant's hand, it seems, immediately
after the despatch of his own instructions to Perponcher ; but with excellent judgment he took upon
himself to disregard them, and to rely upon his own
reading of the situation. Wellington with perfect
coolness explained the state of affairs to his superior
officers, and, after bidding them all withdraw as
quietly and speedily as possible to their posts, left the
ball at two o'clock and went to bed. He was awakened
two or three hours later by General Dörnberg, who
had ridden in from Mons, and to whom he gave
instructions to hasten at once to Mont St. Jean and
order Picton's division forward to Quatre Bras.
Thanks to the foresight of Constant, that important
point on the road of communication between the two

75

1815.  Allied armies was temporarily secure ; and, with the
June 16. rest of his force at Nivelles, Braine-le-Comte and
Enghien, the Duke was prepared to meet attack either
on the direct road from Charleroi to Brussels or further
to westward between Charleroi and Mons.    But
towards seven o'clock Wellington decided definitely
that Quatre Bras was his true point of concentration,
and issued further instructions for a continued eastward movement of the whole army upon that village,
Genappe and Nivelles.  Though it was still uncertain
whether the French advance along the road from
Charleroi to Brussels was made in any force, it was
clear that, in any case, the Anglo-Netherlandish army
must be at hand to support the Prussians if Napoleon's
attack should be delivered against them.

The main significance of the reports brought in
to Napoleon on the night of the 15th was that the
Prussians had retired eastward, and the outposts of
Wellington's army towards the north.  He judged
therefore that his primary object was attained.  He
had placed his own army between the two Allied
hosts, and he was free to fall upon whichever of them
he pleased to select.  He had already decided that,
of the twain, it would be preferable to attack first that
of Blücher, whose fiery temperament would prompt
him to fly to the succour of Wellington, whereas the
British General, whom he judged to be slow and
circumspect, would be less eager to march to the
support of his Prussian colleague.  It is characteristic
of Napoleon that it never occurred to him that two
commanders might act with unselfish loyalty towards
each other.  Good faith, upon principle and not for
personal advantage, was a matter that lay beyond his
horizon : he had always lied to his generals in Spain
and they had always lied to him.[1]  Had he been

[1] On the evening of this same 15th of June he had issued a bulletin
claiming in one passage that the day's operations had cost the Prussians
2600 men, of which 1000 prisoners : and in another that 400 to 500
men had been sabred and 1750 captured—all at a cost to the French
of 10 killed and 80 wounded.  *Corres. de Napoléon*, 22056.

concerned with Gneisenau instead of with Blücher, his diagnosis of character would have been less incorrect; for Gneisenau was equally ignorant of the meaning of good faith, so much so, indeed, that the mere study of his character has infected one of his biographers with the same failing.  However, having made this false assumption, Napoleon built his plan of campaign upon it.  At four o'clock in the morning he sent an officer to Frasnes to learn how affairs stood in that quarter ; and an hour later Soult despatched orders to Ney to ascertain the exact position of Reille's and d'Erlon's corps.  Before eight o'clock the Emperor formulated his plan of operations for the day.  Grouchy and the right wing were to march north-eastward upon Sombreffe and Gembloux, and to fall upon any Prussian corps that might be found in either position.  Gérard's corps might be called in, if needed, for the attack on Sombreffe ;  but the Emperor did not expect to be opposed by more than forty thousand Prussians.  He himself would reach Fleurus between ten and eleven o'clock, leave the whole of his Guard there, and push on alone to Sombreffe.  Having ascertained that Sombreffe and Gembloux were clear of the enemy, he would lead his reserve to join the left wing at Quatre Bras, from whence both united would make a night march northward and by seven o'clock in the morning of the 17th should have reached Brussels. He impressed upon Ney the importance of occupying Brussels, which, as he reckoned, might produce great results ;  for so prompt and sudden a march would isolate the British from Mons and Ostend.

These orders show that on the morning of the 16th Napoleon's ideas of the whereabouts of his enemy were of the vaguest.  He evidently did not expect to find Blücher in force either at Sombreffe or at Gembloux, and, supposing that his expectations proved to be correct, he considered it safe to infer that the Prussians had withdrawn to a secure distance eastward, and that he could devote his principal attention to Wellington.

Equally he expected to find the British in retreat. In the supplementary orders sent by Soult to Ney, it was enjoined upon the latter to occupy Quatre Bras with two corps of infantry and one of cavalry, push on a division of infantry and some cavalry to Genappe, and send out reconnaissances towards Brussels and Nivelles, upon which latter point the Anglo-Netherlanders would probably have retreated.   In other words, he looked that the bare terror of his advance between them should have caused both of their armies to retreat, each towards its own base, in opposite directions, which was the very thing that Blücher and Wellington had agreed not to do.   Against this inference, however, must be set the remarkable allusion to Mons and Ostend in the letter to Ney ; for, if the British were retiring to the west, it is very clear that a rapid advance from Quatre Bras to Brussels would isolate them from neither the one place nor the other.   Indeed, if Wellington, upon the news of Ney's rapid advance, should face about and march eastward, he would fall full upon the Emperor's flank. On the other hand, if we assume that the advance to Brussels was deliberately conceived with the idea of cutting Wellington's communications to westward, then obviously Napoleon expected the Anglo-Netherlandish army to be at Brussels or to east of it.   In that case Wellington's purpose was not to be mistaken. He intended to sacrifice his line of operations with Ostend rather than his contact with the Prussian army ; and, as we have seen, the Duke had promised Gneisenau that he would take this course in the event of a retreat. Had some inkling of this promise and of Wellington's extreme anxiety to preserve Brussels and Ghent reached the Emperor's ears ?   If it had, and if he really believed that the Duke had retired north and eastward, then evidently his plan of falling upon the Allied armies in detail and beating them separately was already wrecked.   Meanwhile, he was for the present too prudent to take anything unverified for granted.

He told Ney plainly that his final decision could not be made until the afternoon or evening, after he had explored the ground as far as Gembloux ; and he bade the Marshal post a division at Marbais, as a central point between Quatre Bras, Sombreffe and Gembloux, so that he could summon it to the support of the right wing in case of need.    Moreover, the division at Marbais was instructed to throw out reconnaissances in every direction, particularly towards Gembloux and even towards Wavre, the latter place being nearly fourteen miles due north of Sombreffe. This indicates that the Emperor kept in view the possibility that the two Allied armies might make a convergent retreat towards the north.    In fact, he was utterly in the dark as to the actual positions and intentions of his enemies ;  and his conjectures were founded upon the false hypothesis that the defeat which he had inflicted upon the Prussians was so serious as to make retreat the only possible course for both armies.

On the evening of the 15th the Prussian army was still for the most part far from its point of concentration, the IInd Corps being between Mazy and Onoz, and the Vth near Namur ;  but orders had been sent to hasten them forward, and some of them were on march during the night.    The IVth corps was hopelessly out of reach.    Gneisenau had sent Bülow only a polite request, instead of a positive order, to move to Hannut on the 15th ;  and the latter General, ignorant that hostilities had begun, ignorant that a general concentration of the army was in progress, and thinking that, if it were, it would take place at Hannut, made no speed to arrive at the place betimes, and was still far east of it when night fell.    Fresh orders were despatched by Blücher to Hannut late in the forenoon of the 15th, bidding Bülow hasten to Gembloux at the earliest possible hour on the 16th ; but, as Bülow was not at Hannut, the letter did not reach him until hard upon midnight, when he returned the inevitable answer, that it was physically impossible for his corps to reach Gembloux at the appointed time.    At about the same hour Gneisenau recalled Ziethen's corps from Fleurus to Sombreffe, and by eight o'clock in the morning of the 16th it was assembled in position between St. Amand and Ligny ; the IInd and IIIrd Corps being still far in rear.    By that time it is to be presumed that Müffling's last letter from Brussels had come to Blücher's hand ;  and at half-past ten there reached him a note from a Prussian aide-de-camp, who had been sent at five o'clock in the morning to Quatre Bras, reporting that the French were still at Frasnes and that their patrols had interrupted communication between the two armies for a time during the night, but that the Prince of Orange expected the whole of the Netherlandish army and most of the British to be concentrated near Nivelles by ten o'clock.    At about eleven o'clock Pirch I.'s corps came up and was placed provisionally between the Roman road and Sombreffe ;  and an hour later Thielmann's corps likewise presented itself and was arrayed on the left of Pirch's from Sombreffe to Tongrinne.    The total force thus assembled numbered about eighty-two thousand men with two hundred and twenty-four guns.

The Prince of Orange, meanwhile, had left Brussels in haste and reached his head-quarters at Braine-le-Comte at half-past three.    After a few words with Constant he confirmed all the orders given by the Chief of his Staff, who then rode off to Quatre Bras. Acting with a strength of initiative not less admirable than Constant's own, Perponcher had kept Prince Bernhard's brigade in its former station and had brought down half of his 2nd brigade, Bijlandt's, to support it.    On his way Constant sent forward Bijlandt's two remaining battalions and artillery from Nivelles to join their division, and on reaching Quatre Bras found Perponcher already engaged in making his dispositions and in driving back the French advanced posts.    At six o'clock the Prince of Orange arrived

and, by Perponcher's advice, extended his front to
give a greater appearance of strength.    He sent
Constant to Nivelles to look to the disposition of
Chassé's division and of Alten's which, once again
through the initiative of Constant, had been bidden
to continue its march from Soignies to Nivelles.    He
also despatched orders to the Guards to continue their
march from Braine-le-Comte to the same place—
orders which miscarried, for Cooke did not receive
them until he reached Nivelles in the afternoon,
having proceeded thither by his own motion.    In the
course of these proceedings Blücher's aide-de-camp
arrived and was sent back with the answer which has
already been quoted ; and at seven o'clock the Prince
reported his proceedings to Wellington, adding that
the French were at Frasnes, with both infantry and
cavalry, but not as yet in force.    There was in fact
nothing so far to show that the French advance upon
the road to Brussels might not after all be a feint, dis-
guising a turning movement further to the west.

So the morning of the 16th wore on.    At nine
o'clock the Allies had still only six thousand five
hundred men and eight guns at Quatre Bras ; and
shortly after that hour Wellington arrived.    From some
stragglers of Steinmetz's brigade he at length learned
some details of what had happened on the previous
day, how the French had crossed the Sambre at
Charleroi and Marchienne, had driven Ziethen back
after sharp encounters at Fleurus and Gosselies, and
had penetrated by patrols as far as the road between
Sombreffe and Quatre Bras.    He appeared surprised
and indeed incredulous, as well he might, for not the
slightest report of these things had been sent to him
from any Prussian source ; but he congratulated the
Prince of Orange and Perponcher upon their courage
in acting upon their own judgment, and approved
their dispositions in every particular.    Riding forward
to reconnoitre for himself, he found that he could see
nothing owing to woods and folds of ground, and, as

1815.
June 16.
the Prince of Orange had no cavalry with him, the Duke was obliged to be content with conjecture. At half-past ten, having at last ascertained the whereabouts of Blücher, he wrote him a letter to the effect that the Prince of Orange's corps was at Quatre Bras and Nivelles, that the Reserve and the British cavalry were on march and would reach Genappe and Nivelles at noon, that Hill was at Braine-le-Comte, that he himself could perceive no great force of the enemy before him, and that he awaited news from the Prussian head-quarters and the arrival of his troops before deciding upon the day's operations. This intelligence, supplied to Wellington by his staff, was very inaccurate, as the subsequent narrative will prove ; but the Duke furnished it in good faith and based his own actions upon the assumed truth of it. The insinuations of German writers, that he wrote this letter with the deliberate purpose of deceiving Blücher and making him fight a battle to cover the concentration of the Anglo-Netherlandish army, deserve nothing more than contempt.[1]

[1] It is a pity that General Pollio (French translation, pp. 197-8) should write : " Sortons du champ des suppositions—Wellington était peut-être plus diplomate que général, il faisait partie du cabinet anglais bien qu'éloigné de Londres, il occupait une position très élevée, supérieure à celle de Blücher, et il s'attribuait en outre une telle supériorité dans son orgueil brittannique qu'il a probablement cru agir avec Blücher comme il avait agi dans la Péninsule avec ses alliés portugais et espagnols." It is well when quitting the domain of conjecture at least not to exchange it for that of fiction, not to say falsehood. Wellington was certainly an able diplomatist, but he did not base his diplomacy upon deceit, as General Pollio quite gratuitously assumes. He was not a member of the British Cabinet, to which he seldom wrote more acrimonious letters than during this short campaign. Finally, any one conversant with the history of the Peninsular war (which no foreigner is, and General Pollio very manifestly is not) would know that, even if it were true that Wellington endeavoured to save himself by deceiving Blücher, no parallel case could be adduced from his relations with the Spaniards and Portuguese. General Pollio evidently is not even aware that the Portuguese troops were commanded by a British General, paid by the British Treasury, and mingled in every division with British troops—a pretty critic to pronounce judgment on Wellington whether as General, diplomatist or man.

Shortly afterwards the Duke rode on with Müffling
to Ligny to see Blücher.  He met the old Field-
marshal near Brye on the right of the chosen battle-
field, where the troops were already forming for the
combat ; and he observed with astonishment that they
were so arrayed on the forward slope of the hill that
no cannon-shot could help striking the supports and
reserves, even if it should miss the fighting line.  He
protested mildly.  " Every man knows his own troops
best," he hinted ;  " but if my troops were so disposed
I should expect them to be beaten."  Such criticism,
however gently advanced, was not likely to commend
itself to a theorist such as Gneisenau, who, besides, was
more concerned with the help that Wellington might
be able to afford him than with his own dispositions.
The Duke, who was still inclined to think that the
French were only making a demonstration before
Frasnes, had, during the ride to Ligny, declared to
Müffling his willingness to bring his whole force, if
possible, to the assistance of the Prussians ;  and,
though no record of his conversation with Blücher is
preserved, there can be no doubt that he repeated to
the Field-marshal the substance of the words which
he had already used to the attaché.  From the mill of
Bussy, which commanded a great extent of ground,
the French columns could be seen advancing to the
attack ; and Gneisenau, thinking that practically the
whole French army was before him, urged the Duke
to bring as large a force as possible to Brye to act as
a reserve to the Prussian army.  Wellington, supported by Müffling, was inclined rather to overthrow
the French force before him at Quatre Bras and march
on Gosselies, that is to say upon the rear of the main
French army.  The discussion was closed by Wellington, who said, " Well, I will come, if I am not
attacked myself " ;  and therewith he started to ride
back to Quatre Bras.  It was then apparently between
half-past one and two o'clock.

Let us return now to the French side.  Ney received

1815.
June 16.

in succession Napoleon's own order and Soult's, which was to the same effect, somewhere about eleven o'clock. He answered at that hour that he was making his dispositions accordingly, that there appeared to be only three thousand infantry and a very few cavalry in his front, and that, in his opinion, there would be little obstacle in the way of the Emperor's dispositions for the march on Brussels. Meanwhile Napoleon, having given Grouchy his orders and summoned Gérard to bring the whole of his corps across the Sambre and lead it straight upon Sombreffe, prepared to ride to Fleurus. Just before he started he received, apparently some time before ten o'clock, a message from the left wing, stating that the enemy was showing considerable strength at Quatre Bras ; whereupon he forwarded to Ney through Soult the following order, which was little more than a confirmation of those already despatched. "Assemble Reille's and d'Erlon's corps, and Kellermann's, which will march to join you at once. With these you should be able to defeat and destroy any force of the enemy that might present themselves. Blücher was at Namur yesterday, and is not likely to have sent troops to Quatre Bras, so you will have none but those that come from Brussels to deal with." Here again we meet with the same confusion of thought as appears in Napoleon's first order already quoted. What did he mean by "the force coming from Brussels ? " Why should no hostile force come up from the west ? Or, if the British at large were retiring westward, why should they march southward from Brussels at all, when they could join the general retreat by moving by the great road to Ninove ? On the other hand, if a French advance upon Brussels was to cut the British off from the base at Ostend, obviously the bulk of the British force must be to east or north-east of Brussels, in which case their movement southward from the capital might be very formidable. But still more remarkable is the fact that the purport of the message delivered to

Napoleon as to the strength of the Allies at Quatre
Bras must have been made known to Ney before he
wrote his answer to the Emperor's first orders, and
that, having once declared the force at that village to
be trifling, he was at no pains to contradict it.   The
French commanders one and all seem to have based
their plans upon hypotheses which they took not the
slightest pains to verify by reconnaissance.

At about eleven o'clock Napoleon reached Fleurus
and, ascending to the summit of a mill, surveyed
Blücher's position at Ligny.   He reckoned correctly
that he had only one corps before him, though there
were signs already of the approach of others, and
resolved to attack at once, but was annoyed to find
that Gérard's corps had not come up.   Soult had sent
off his orders to Gérard between seven and eight
o'clock, but they seem to have taken two hours to
travel four miles, for they did not come to hand until
half-past nine, or at any rate Gérard did not set his
troops in motion until that hour.   It was then necessary for them to defile across the narrow bridge at
Châtelet, and thus it was half-past one before they
reached the field of action.   At two o'clock the
Emperor sent through Soult a fourth message to Ney,
which conditionally cancelled the previous instructions
respecting the march to Brussels.   Its purport was
that the Prussians had assembled a corps between
Sombreffe and Brye, which would be attacked by
Grouchy with the 3rd and 4th Corps at half-past
two.   Ney was therefore required to drive back with
vigour whatever hostile troops might be in front of
him, and, having done so, to fall back towards the
right wing so as to envelop the Prussians aforesaid.
If, on the other hand, the Emperor should have already
defeated them, he would manœuvre in Ney's direction
to hasten the accomplishment of the operations prescribed to the Marshal.

At three o'clock Napoleon's dispositions were
complete and he ordered the attack to begin.   He

had at his disposal the 3rd and 4th Corps (Vandamme's and Gérard's), Girard's division of Reille's
corps, Lobau's corps, which was ordered forward
from Charleroi just as the battle began, also Pajol's,
Exelmans's and Milhaud's corps of cavalry, in
all seventy-six thousand men, or deducting Lobau's
corps, which was not actually on the spot, sixty-five
thousand men.    By this time Napoleon was alive to
the fact that he had before him not a corps but an
army ;  but he was elated rather than depressed by
the fact, for he asked nothing better than to have
done with Blücher at a stroke.    " The issue of this
war may be decided in three hours," he said.    " If
Ney executes my orders properly, not a gun of this
army will escape ";  and therewith he despatched to
Ney a fifth set of instructions.    " We are heavily
engaged with the Prussians " (such was its purport),
" manœuvre at once so as to envelope their right and
fall with clenched fists upon their rear.    If you act
with vigour this army of theirs is lost.    The fate of
France is in your hands.    Lose not a moment in
marching on the heights of St. Amand and Brye, to
share in what may be a decisive victory."    These
instructions completely ignored the possibility that
Ney might have an enemy in front of him ;  and, just
at the moment, as it happened, a letter reached the
Emperor from Lobau, telling him that Ney was confronted with twenty thousand men at Quatre Bras.
The news did not disconcert Napoleon.    If Ney could
not spare his whole army, he must hold the enemy
before him in check with Reille's corps only, and
send d'Erlon's to make the turning movement upon
Blücher's right.    Napoleon accordingly sent an order
to this effect to Ney.

The battle of Ligny forms no part of the history
of the British army, and only the briefest summary of
its course can be given here.    Napoleon opened the
fight by a vigorous attack upon Blücher's right and
centre, which was met by as strenuous a defence, and

by counter-attacks which were resisted by the French
with a stubbornness equal to that of the Prussians
themselves.   After more than two hours of a bitter
struggle no ground had been gained by either party ;
and, since Lobau's corps was now approaching, Napoleon resolved to launch the Guard to a supreme attack
against the Prussian centre ;  hoping to cleave the
army in twain, surround the right wing with the help
of d'Erlon, and drive the left wing eastward upon
Namur.   The dispositions had been made and the
attack was about to begin when the Emperor was
informed that a strong hostile column was bearing
down upon his left flank, and in fact that the French
troops in that quarter were falling back in disorder,
or, in plain words, running away.   Perforce he suspended the assault of his Guard and sent half of them
to strengthen the threatened flank.   Blücher seized
the moment to aim a great counter-stroke at the
French left.   He was, however, repulsed, and presently the Emperor learned that the supposed hostile
column was d'Erlon's corps.   So intense seems to
have been his relief at this welcome tidings that he
forgot everything else in the renewal of his attack upon
the Prussian centre ;  while d'Erlon, who had just
received a pressing order from Ney to return to Quatre
Bras, counter-marched and left the field of Ligny
behind him.

By about seven o'clock all was ready ; and after a
heavy cannonade the Guard were let loose to the assault.
Blücher, having already used up his reserves on his
right, had little infantry with which to meet them.
The gallant old warrior therefore led his reserve cavalry
in person to the charge, but his troops could make
no impression upon the Guard, and were repulsed
with great loss.   His horse was shot under him, and
while on the ground he was ridden over and trampled
on, only escaping at last on a sergeant's horse,
bruised, shaken, and hardly conscious.   The whole
of the Prussian centre broke up in disorder, and

1815. the battle was lost.    Sixty-five thousand French had
June 16. beaten eighty-three thousand Prussians, through the
fault, not of the Prussian rank and file, but of Gneisenau
and his colleagues of the staff, who had chosen a very
defective position in the first place and defended it
very unskilfully in the second.    With a superiority of
nearly four to three they should certainly have given
a better account of Napoleon ; and it is childish to
contend, as German writers have with unblushing
effrontery contended, that Blücher would not have
accepted battle had he not counted upon help from
Wellington.    Blücher was firmly resolved to fight in
any circumstances ; [1] and, if his tactical skill had been
equal to his courage and constancy, the result would
amply have justified his determination.

On the French left wing Ney, apparently confident
that he would meet with little resistance at Quatre
Bras, made no preparations for an advance before
receiving the Emperor's commands.    Nor were these,
as we have seen, at the outset of a nature to demand
particular activity or haste, since they gave him to
understand that no serious work would be expected
of him before nightfall.    He issued therefore no orders
for the march of his infantry upon the road to Brussels
until eleven o'clock, which signified that Reille's
divisions were not fairly in movement before noon, and
that the head of the column did not reach Frasnes
until half-past one.    At this spot there were already
Bachelu's division, about five thousand men, Piré's
and Lefebvre-Desnoëttes's light cavalry, rather under
four thousand men, and twenty-six guns.

The hamlet of Quatre Bras lies at the intersection
of the roads that lead from Brussels to Charleroi and
from Nivelles to Namur, at a point about two and a
half miles due north of Frasnes.    On an elevation,
slightly higher than the undulating ground on every
side, stood a very large farm-house and buildings, with
a few labourers' cottages, all clustered about the actual

[1] See James, p. 113.

cross-roads. To westward of the cross the Namur road passes through a deep cutting to an embankment, and to eastward from an embankment to a cutting, forming in either case a natural line of defence. From the farm the ground slopes gently southward along the Brussels road to a tiny rivulet which, rising about five hundred yards west of the road, passed under it, and was dammed up about a thousand yards farther east into a wedge-shaped pond, called the Materne Pond, broadening at its eastern end, and measuring about four hundred yards from east to west. At the foot of the slope which rises southward from this rivulet, and just on the eastern side of the Brussels road, stood another farm, that of Gemioncourt ; and from the rivulet itself, which likewise bears the name of Gemioncourt, the ground ascends gently for some six hundred yards and ripples away southward towards Frasnes, throwing out, however, within eleven hundred yards of Gemioncourt, a well-marked spur to the east, which is defined along its southern flank by a second small rivulet, whose course is parallel to that of Gemioncourt. Near the eastern extremity of this spur and about three-quarters of a mile east of the Brussels road stands another group of farm buildings known as Pireaumont farm. West of the road and nearly a mile south-west of Gemioncourt farm, the farm of Grand Pierrepont marks the source of another rivulet, that of Odomont, which flows through a depression in a south-westerly direction, passing a second farm, Petit Pierrepont, some eight hundred yards on its downward course. The other main features of the ground were two woods of considerable extent, of which the first, Hutte Wood, extended from a point a little south of Pireaumont for some two thousand yards southward, with a breadth of rather less than a mile east and west. The other wood, that of Bossu, extended west of the Brussels road, practically from Quatre Bras farm to within six hundred yards of Grand Pierrepont, gradually widening out from a

breadth of about five hundred yards by Quatre Bras
to sixteen hundred yards abreast of Gemioncourt, and
then running out into a narrow tongue from the south-
western corner towards Pierrepont.   This Bossu Wood
was of very thick coppice with high but scanty standards, and was traversed by broad rides convenient for
the passage of troops.   North of the Namur road yet
another smaller wood—Bois des Cerises or Cherry
Wood—stretched from the road itself opposite to the
Materne Pond almost to the village of Sart-Dame-
Avelines.   Round the buildings there were orchards
and gardens ;  on the borders of the stream were little
thickets and rows of trees ; and the open country was
covered with tall crops of corn.   Altogether the
position was blind, and, in the hands of a capable commander, well susceptible of defence ;  though the
Hutte Wood effectively screened the movements of an
enemy coming up from the south on the eastern side
of the Brussels road.

Guided by the advice of Perponcher, the Prince of
Orange extended one battalion in skirmishing order
along the spur between the rivulets of Gemioncourt
and Pireaumont to the Brussels road, and thence south-
westward along the Odomont rivulet; the farms of
Pireaumont and Petit Pierrepont forming the two
extremities of the line to left and right, with one
battery upon the road in the centre.   Next in rear of
them four battalions were stationed near the southern
border of Bossu Wood, with two more battalions, also
in the wood, in support.   Another battery was posted
at the south-eastern angle of the wood, and between
it and Gemioncourt farm, which was strongly occupied ;
and three more battalions were echeloned along the
road from Quatre Bras farm to Gemioncourt.   In all,
at two o'clock the Prince had at his disposal about
seven thousand men with sixteen guns ;  and at three
o'clock the arrival of another battalion, which had
been released from Nivelles by the coming of Chassé's
and Alten's divisions to that place, increased his number

to nearly eight thousand.    To hold a good two miles
of front with so weak a detachment could not but be
hazardous ; but it was imperative for the moment to
make a show of strength ; and every credit must be
given to Perponcher for the bold face with which he
confronted a critical situation.

At about two o'clock the head of Bachelu's division
—Husson's brigade—under the personal direction of
Reille, debouched on to the plateau at the north-western
corner of Hutte Wood.    Ney, with Piré's light cavalry
of the line and Lefebvre-Desnoëttes's of the Guard,
was already on the ground, and had ridden forward
with a single aide-de-camp to reconnoitre.    Unable to
see many troops, he concluded that the position was
weakly held, and was for assailing Bossu Wood without
delay.    Reille, however, who had observed the scarlet
uniforms of British officers, remembered Wellington's
custom of hiding his men, and pleaded that more
battalions should be brought up before opening the
attack.    There was therefore a pause, whilst Bachelu's
second brigade and Foy's division came forward to
the plateau, when four columns were formed and
directed upon the spur between Pireaumont and the
Brussels road.    On the extreme right or east were
Piré's division of cavalry, next to the left of it were
the two brigades of Bachelu's division, Campy's on the
right and Husson's on the left ; and the left column
of all was made up of Jamin's brigade of Foy's
division.    Gauthier's brigade, together with the cavalry
of Lefebvre-Desnoëttes and Guiton's cuirassiers were
held in reserve on the road.    The rest of Kellermann's
cavalry corps, to which Guiton's brigade belonged,
had been stationed by Ney at Liberchies, about two
miles south-west of Frasnes.    Jerome's division of
infantry was on the march from Gosselies, and d'Erlon's
corps was following in rear of it.    Altogether Ney
could reckon that he had thirty-five thousand infantry,
seven thousand cavalry, and ninety-two guns under
his hand or within easy call, of which he had detached

1815. for his first attack about six thousand infantry, two
June 16. thousand cavalry, and six guns.

Before the advance of numbers so overwhelming
the Netherlandish skirmishers fell back towards
Gemioncourt, where Perponcher installed them in
and about the buildings ; and the Prince of Orange
withdrew the two batteries from their advanced
positions to a knoll a short distance south of Quatre
Bras from which they could rake the Brussels road.
Foy then changed the direction of his column to the
left, and drove the Netherlanders from Gemioncourt.
These retreated hastily up the road, but were unlucky
enough to be charged and utterly dispersed by Piré,
who, finding his way obstructed by boggy ground,
had returned to the highway.   Meanwhile the head
of Jerome's column came up, releasing Gauthier's
brigade and enabling Ney to press the Netherlanders back from Pierrepont into Bossu Wood.
There the French could advance but slowly, for the
undergrowth was exceedingly thick, and the Netherlanders offered some resistance.   Nevertheless the
enemy mastered the borders of the wood and pressed
their opponents surely and steadily backward.   Let
Netherlandish writers say what they will, the initial
efforts of their comrades do not appear to have been
very strenuous on this day.   The advanced posts
were not held with the tenacity which the occasion
demanded, and the troops did not respond as they
ought to the leadership of the gallant young Prince
and the brave and skilful General who were at their
head.

They were now, however, in great measure to
redeem their character.   Wellington had returned
from Ligny; and soon after two o'clock the leading
battalions of Picton's division came into sight,[1]
Kempt's brigade leading, and the Ninety-fifth, apparently, at the head of the column.   Van Merlen's

[1] Accounts vary as to the time when Picton's division came up.
The head of the column must have come in about 2 P.M.

brigade of Netherlandish cavalry arrived at almost the same moment, and the legion of the Duke of Brunswick was following close in the rear of Picton. In the desperate situation of the moment Wellington saw no salvation but in a counter-attack.[1] He therefore directed the Riflemen to move at once upon Pireaumont and to endeavour to regain it, but at all events to secure Cherry Wood so as to ensure the safety of the Namur road and so of communication with the Prussian army. At the same time he ordered the Netherlanders to recover Gemioncourt and sent the Twenty-eighth down to help to hold the buildings. The remainder of Picton's division was diverted round the east side of Quatre Bras, with instructions to align itself along the Namur road, the Ninety-second forming the right of the line with its right resting on the buildings, and then in succession upon its left, the Forty-second, Forty-fourth, Royal Scots, Thirty-second and Seventy-ninth,[2] with Rogers's battery of artillery on the right and Rettberg's on the left of the array. Best's Hanoverian brigade[3] was ordered to stand in second line behind the British battalions. On the right Prince Bernhard, likewise, was bidden to make a counter-attack and to clear Bossu Wood of the enemy.

These dispositions required some time for their execution, for it was long before the last of the regiments arrived ; and meanwhile the Riflemen, before they were half-way to Pireaumont, saw the enemy throw so powerful a force into the farm as to make attack hopeless. Another body of French was pushing on towards Cherry Wood, but here the Riflemen

1815.
June 16.

---

[1] The true significance of this counter-attack is missed, as it seems to me, by all writers except Müffling. Wellington, *Supp. Desp.* x. 511.

[2] This order is conjectural. It is, however, certain that the 92nd was on the extreme right and the 79th on the extreme left, also (*Waterloo Letters*, p. 377) that the 42nd was on the right of the 44th instead of on the left, as it should have been.

[3] This brigade belonged to the Reserve and not to Picton's division at all ; but by some mistake had been sent forward with it.

anticipated them, and, throwing their reserve into the wood, lined the road with their skirmishers and engaged the enemy hotly. Gradually the green‑jackets extended their line down the road to the hamlet of Thyle, where two companies ensconced themselves in the houses and for the present secured their left flank. In the centre the Dutch Militia recovered Gemioncourt, and deploying in front of the farm beat off an attack of the French cavalry; but, finding themselves outflanked by the advance of Foy on their right, they were obliged to evacuate the buildings once more. The British Twenty-eighth, seeing that it had arrived too late, thereupon counter-marched and returned to their division. Prince Bernhard, on his side, took the offensive with great spirit in Bossu Wood, drove the French with the bayonet from a part that they had taken, and, with the help of a fresh battalion sent to him by the Prince of Orange, made shift to maintain the advantage that he had won.

Wellington's counter-stroke had at least gained time for Picton to set his division in order, and for part of the Duke of Brunswick's legion to reach the scene of action; though it had failed to recover the important posts on his centre and left. The possession of Gemioncourt and of the skirts of Bossu Wood enabled Ney to bring forward his whole army without further interruption; and, as he appears to have received at about this time Soult's letter bidding him drive his enemy back and then swing round to attack the Prussians at Brye, he launched his attack along the whole line in earnest. Sixteen guns were massed to east of the Brussels road, and twenty-six between Pireaumont and Gemioncourt. On his right Bachelu advanced from Pireaumont against the troops on the Namur road; in his centre Foy led his division in two columns along the Brussels road and to the east of it upon Quatre Bras; and on the left Jerome threw Soye's brigade into Bossu Wood and led Bauduin's brigade parallel with Foy's division on the western side of the road. A heavy cannonade heralded the onslaught, and it should seem that Bachelu's division was the first to come to close action, for his sharp-shooters were already working deadly mischief among the British gunners before more than the leading section of Rogers's battery had come into action. The bulk of Picton's division was hidden among the dense crops of rye which covered the fields, and the skirmishers of both sides were hotly engaged, when Wellington suddenly ordered Kempt's brigade to rise and advance. Whether dismayed by the unexpected apparition, or shaken by the British volley, Bachelu's leading regiment, the 2nd Light, broke and fled without awaiting the charge,[1] and the whole division, turning tail, rushed down the hill to the Gemioncourt rivulet and would not be rallied even on the plateau beyond it.

Most of the British battalions pursued no farther than to a hedge at a short distance from the Namur road; but the Forty-second and Forty-fourth advanced to within a short distance of Gemioncourt, and the Seventy-ninth, which by Wellington's order had begun the offensive movement before the rest of the battalions, pressed the chase to the rivulet and even beyond it. Foy, however, observing the rout of Bachelu, had withdrawn the 100th regiment from Jamin's brigade, and, after bidding that officer continue his advance to Quatre Bras, had betaken himself with the 100th to the plateau south of Gemioncourt. It was he who arrested the career of the three battalions, though the Seventy-ninth, taking shelter behind a fence, fired volleys at the 100th until its ammunition was exhausted. Not for some time did the Camerons retire, when, on receiving orders to fall back, they stole warily from fence to fence and, covered by the

---

[1] This is the account given by Foy, *Girod de l'Ain*, p. 271. He says that four British battalions charged; but the 95th was still detached from Kempt's brigade, so that there can have been only three.

Thirty-second, regained without serious loss their original position.   From a few of the most headlong of the Seventy-ninth, whom he made prisoners, Foy learned that eight British brigades had just come in from Enghien and Brussels, and that others besides Netherlanders were on march to Quatre Bras.   This intelligence he no doubt transmitted to Ney.

On the French left the progress of Soye in Bossu Wood was immediate ; raw troops, such as the Netherlanders, having little chance in forest-fighting against veterans ; and Wellington, in order to guard their left flank and give them confidence, sent two Brunswick battalions down the road to a point midway between Quatre Bras and Gemioncourt, stationing the Brunswick cavalry immediately behind them. Lastly, he posted two more battalions in the corner of the wood adjoining Quatre Bras with orders to fight to the last extremity.   The foremost of these troops soon suffered heavily from the fire of a French battery on the road above Gemioncourt ; and four British guns, which the Duke of Brunswick had borrowed from Wellington and unlimbered by his infantry, were quickly silenced.   Shortly afterwards the columns of Jamin, Gauthier and Bauduin approached on both sides of the road, and both Brunswickers and Netherlanders gradually gave way before them.   The Duke of Brunswick, taking command of his squadron of lancers, charged the advancing French to cover the retreat of his infantry and hussars, but was beaten back with heavy loss.   The lancers fled to the rear of Quatre Bras, whither the hussars also retired in more orderly fashion.   One of Brunswick's regiments of infantry, under his personal command, struck eastward from the Brussels road towards Picton's division, but the other, harried by the pursuing French skirmishers and by the round-shot of the French batteries, broke and fled in all directions.   The Duke of Brunswick, hurrying back, tried to rally them under cover of a house and garden called the Bergerie, upon the road

about three hundred yards south of Quatre Bras, but 1815.
fell mortally wounded by a bullet through the body. June 16.
Now Piré's cavalry, two regiments of chasseurs
leading and two regiments of lancers in rear, came
galloping up the road to complete their success ;
and the Brunswick Hussars were formed again to
meet them, together, it appears, with Van Merlen's
cavalry, which had been hastily ordered to the front
by the Prince of Orange.   Both were overthrown and
put to flight without difficulty by the chasseurs and they
streamed away, some straight up the Brussels road to
Quatre Bras, some eastward towards the Namur road.
The chasseurs, close at the heels of the former,
flew up the highway after them, while the lancers,
wheeling sharply to their right, took up the chase of
those that had turned east ;  and pursuers and pursued
in a mixed body crowded into the angle between the
two roads.

The Ninety-second, which was the last of Picton's
battalions to come up, had not long taken up their
position, under Wellington's own eye, immediately on
the east side of Quatre Bras ; the men lying down in
the ditch on the south side of the Namur road to gain
shelter from the fire of the French batteries in their
front.   As the chasseurs approached them the Duke,
who was watching the fight a short distance in front
of the Highlanders, was obliged to turn and gallop for
his life ; and, crying to the men to lie still, he put his
horse at the ditch, leaped over them, and took his place
in rear of the regiment.   As the leading files of the
chasseurs whirled up the Brussels road, the right-
hand company of the Ninety-second wheeled round
parallel to it and poured a destructive fire upon their
right flank, while the Brunswickers in the north-
eastern angle of Bossu Wood simultaneously rained
bullets upon their left flank.   This cross-fire fairly
cut the column of the chasseurs in twain.   The rearmost rallied and retired in good order, but the foremost
pressed on into the village and beyond it, cutting down

stragglers and fugitives; when, finding themselves
unable to retreat by the way of their advance, they
tried to find egress through the buildings or along
the Namur road in rear of the Highlanders, and were
shot down to a man. At this point, therefore, the
onset of the cavalry was checked with heavy loss.

The lancers were more fortunate in their venture.
As they swept past the right flank of the Forty-second
and Forty-fourth, which were standing in line close to
the eastern margin of the Brussels road, they were
so closely intermingled with the Brunswick Hussars
and Belgians that the British at first mistook them
for the Allied cavalry. A few old soldiers did indeed
recognise them as enemies and open fire, but were
sternly repressed by Pack ; and the lancers, then
wheeling about, charged down upon the rear of the
British regiments. The Forty-second, having had a
closer view of the cavalry than the Forty-fourth,
realised their danger and began to form square, but,
before the two flank-companies could run in to close
the rear face, the lancers overtook them and, by the
impetus of their charge, some few of them crashed into
the mass of the battalion. For a moment there was
some confusion. The senior officers sprang forward
to rally the Highlanders, and in a few minutes the
Colonel, second and third in command were dead.
Then the flank-companies closed in, the square was
completed, and the lancers, who had at first broken in,
found themselves imprisoned and were bayoneted or
taken to a man. The rest were driven off by the
musketry of the remaining faces of the square with
very heavy loss. Meanwhile the Colonel of the Forty-
fourth, seeing that there was no time to form square,
faced his rear rank about, and, waiting till the enemy
was within close range, gave them a volley which
emptied many saddles and effectually checked the rest.
One little knot of daring Frenchmen, however, made a
gallant dash for the colours, which were as gallantly
defended ; and, though the precious silk was actually

torn by the point of a French lance, not a fragment became a trophy to the enemy.    Meanwhile the
bulk of the lancers fled round the left flank of the
battalion, receiving a volley from the light company
as they passed, and were saluted by another discharge
from the front rank before they finally disappeared.
Let it be added that Colonel Galbois of the 6th French
Lancers received a bullet in the chest during this
encounter, but remained in the saddle and commanded
his regiment two days later at Waterloo.    Never did
British soldiers bear themselves better, and never were
they matched against nobler foemen.

On the whole, Ney's great attack had failed.    He
had been completely repulsed at every point to east of
the Brussels road ; and his attempts to turn the British
left flank had been steadily foiled by the Riflemen,[1]
who, though driven by artillery from their little citadel
at Thyle, continued to defend the Namur road with the
greatest obstinacy.    Only in Bossu Wood, which seems
to have swallowed up the bulk of Jerome's division,[2]
were the French making progress in spite of the
thickness of the undergrowth.    At this point indeed
the resistance of the Netherlanders, as was pardonable
in young troops which had been roughly handled, was
beginning to grow weak ; and, as the Forty-second,
Forty-fourth and Seventy-ninth had suffered very

[1] They had been reinforced by a Brunswick battalion, so raw that
they could not be restrained from firing in all directions, and chiefly at
their friends the Riflemen.

[2] It is exceedingly difficult to follow the movements of the French
infantry in this action.    Soye's brigade of Jerome's division was in
Bossu Wood, but Bauduin's was free to advance between the wood
and the Brussels road.    Of Foy's division, one regiment of Jamin's
brigade was covering the re-formation of Bachelu's division, but the
other should have been advancing parallel with Bauduin's brigade ;
while Gauthier's brigade, albeit repulsed at the outset, should have
been re-forming or re-formed in rear of Jamin.    Apparently all movements of the infantry, except in the wood, were suspended during the
attack of the cavalry ; presumably because the troops to east of the
wood dared not advance until their left flank was cleared.    It seems
probable that these last were for long checked at the re-entrant angle
where the northern end of the wood joins the road.

heavily, being always under the fire of the French artillery, Wellington's situation was not of the securest. But, on the other hand, Ney also was in trouble. Soult's message had arrived reiterating the order to march upon the right flank of Blücher, and warning him that the fate of France was in his hands; and, as if in mockery, there came to his hands almost simultaneously a message carried by the chief of d'Erlon's staff, reporting that by the Emperor's order the 1st Corps was on its way to the battle-field of Ligny. Furious with rage, Ney sent a peremptory order to d'Erlon to return at once, and calling to him Kellermann, told him that the time was come for a great effort, and that he must hurl his cavalry at the British and gallop over them. Possibly the Marshal forgot that three out of four brigades of Kellermann's cavalry corps were at Liberchies, and only one brigade present at Frasnes,[1] and was under the impression that he was about to launch thirty-five hundred men upon the Allied line instead of eight hundred. Be that as it may, Kellermann demurred to the order, pointing out that a single brigade could do little against twenty-five thousand men. " What matter ? " cried Ney. " Charge with whatever you have got. Gallop over them. I'll support you with all the cavalry that I have on the spot. Off with you ! I say, off with you ! "

Kellermann thereupon went to the head of Guiton's brigade and led them at a smart trot down the road ; while the French batteries redoubled their fire upon the British infantry. Arrived at the summit of the plateau north of the Gemioncourt rivulet, he increased his front to a column of squadrons at twice deploying distance, and advanced at a gallop, hurrying his men into action before they could perceive their danger. The first attack was delivered on the east of the road

---

[1] Siborne says that the whole of L'Héritier's division was at Frasnes ; Houssaye says that Guiton's brigade only was engaged, and this is confirmed by the reports both of Ney and of Kellermann. The latter indeed said that he did not know where L'Héritier's division was.

against the Forty-second and Forty-fourth, which,
unable to see anything over the tall stalks of the rye in
which they stood, were warned of the coming wrath
by the inrush of their skirmishers.  By this time both
battalions had been reduced to little more than half
of their original strength, but they formed two tiny
squares with perfect steadiness and awaited the shock.
The horses of the cuirassiers, after a rapid advance of
over a mile, the latter part of the distance through
thick corn as high as their withers, were doubtless
somewhat blown ;  but their riders pressed them
gallantly on almost to the points of the British bayonets.
Then at last the red-coats drew trigger, and the leading
squadron, broken and shattered by the fire, swerved
away and disappeared.  The other squadrons followed
them in wave upon wave, only to meet with the same
fate ;  and then, rallying, they renewed their onset
upon two or more different faces of the squares, striving
desperately but in vain to break into the hedge of
bayonets.  Some of the rear squadrons, meanwhile,
dashed straight on by the road and parallel to it upon
Quatre Bras and the Highlanders who were aligned
to east of it.  " Ninety-second, don't fire till I tell
you ! " shouted Wellington ;  and, waiting until the
enemy were within thirty yards, he gave the word,
when a withering volley sent the daring horsemen
back in confusion.

The cuirassiers then retired to rally[1] under the
shelter of the southern slope of the ridge, leaving the
artillery to play upon the squares.  Being reinforced by
Piré's chasseurs and lancers, they presently renewed
the attack.  Once again there was a wild rush upon
Quatre Bras and once again it was shattered by the

[1] It is extremely difficult to discover how many distinct attacks
were delivered by the French cavalry.  Houssaye treats them all as
one ;  Siborne treats them as two ;  but judging from the narratives
of the British regiments in *Waterloo Letters* I conceive that there were
four, one of cuirassiers only, a second of cuirassiers supported by Piré's
division, and a third and fourth, in one or both of which Lefebvre-
Desnoëtte's division, or a part of it, took some share.

Ninety-second, though a few brave horsemen made their way into the village and one French officer was actually shot in rear of the Highlanders. But the principal onslaught was, as before, upon the Forty-second and Forty-fourth, which were fairly hemmed in and hidden by a mixed multitude of chasseurs, lancers, and cuirassiers, but nevertheless stood indomitably firm and refused to be broken. At last Picton, weary of waiting for the Netherlandish cavalry to come to the front, formed the First Royals and Twenty-eighth in one solid column of companies and advanced with them from the Namur road into the thick of the French horse upon the right of the Forty-fourth. Halting when he had reached a position from which he could bring a flanking fire to bear in favour of the Forty-fourth, he suddenly formed both regiments into one square ; and, the Thirty-second and Seventy-ninth advancing likewise in the same formation to the south of the Royals and Twenty-eighth, the division made up a cluster of five squares drawn up more or less chequerwise for mutual support. At the same time Best's Hanoverian Brigade came forward to line the Namur road, which it did with three battalions, the fourth being pushed somewhat in advance. Against the new squares of red-coats the French turned with undiminished spirit and valour. Unable to see their enemy owing to the height of the rye, some of Piré's troopers fixed their lances in the ground close to the various squares, and upon these marks their comrades charged again and again with desperate but unavailing hardihood. There appears to have been little method in their attacks. There was no crash of squadron after squadron upon one given point, but an endless swirl of horsemen round and round the squares, which, though slightly thinned by occasional lance-thrusts, maintained eternally their deadly rolling fire. Scores of men and horses were brought down ; and at length the French horsemen were again called off, to be rallied and re-formed.

Once more the French guns opened on the squares,
and, worse still, the French sharp-shooters crept up and
began to pour a destructive fire upon them.  Perforce
British skirmishers had to go forward to meet them; but
with so little ammunition that they were at great disadvantage.  At length the last round was exhausted,
and Pack recalled the skirmishers to the squares ; but,
before the order could be executed, the cuirassiers and
lancers were upon them.  Forming into columns of
fours the little band charged through the horsemen,
reached the Forty-fourth and lay down under the
bayonets, the square being so hotly assailed at the
moment that it could not open its ranks even to admit
friends.  The French commanders, evidently endeavouring to improve their tactics, marshalled their
men for a simultaneous attack upon three sides of the
square of the Royals and Twenty-eighth.  Picton uttered
not a word except " Twenty-eighth, remember Egypt,"
and the charge was beaten off, as had been all previous
charges, with heavy loss to the enemy.  Thereupon
the old disorder began afresh, and the attack degene-
rated into a confusion of galloping swarms in and out
of the squares.  At one point, however, it was at last
successful, for a party of lancers surprised Best's
advanced Hanoverian battalion when deployed in line,
and practically destroyed it.  Heartened by this
victory the lancers tried to cross the Namur road, but
were driven back in confusion by the fire of the
remaining battalions which were concealed in a ditch
by the highway.  Then for the third time the French
cavalry was drawn off to re-form ; and the red-coats
were left to the mercy of the cannon and sharp-
shooters of the enemy.

The Forty - second and Forty - fourth were now
formed into a single square under the personal command of Pack ; but, having little ammunition left, they
and the Seventy-ninth were reduced almost to the
limits of their endurance.  Happily at this moment
came up two brigades of Alten's division, Colin

1815.
June 16.
Halkett's British and Kielmansegge's Hanoverians, the former of which was directed by Picton to move down through Bossu Wood and fall upon the French left, and the latter to reinforce the Riflemen on the extreme Allied left. Entering the wood, Halkett encountered an aide-de-camp sent by Pack, who represented that there were few cartridges left in his brigade, and that unless speedily supported he could no longer hold his position. Detaching the Sixty-ninth to the help of Pack, Halkett led the rest of his brigade into the wood just in time to stop the Bruns-wickers, who were on the point of abandoning it. The Brunswickers were not without excuse, for the bulk of the Netherlanders were by this time streaming away in flight along the road to Nivelles.[1] By a few hard words, aided by the presence of his own brigade, Halkett induced them to rally in a ditch which ran across the narrowest part of the wood, and galloped forward to the ground overlooking Gemioncourt to reconnoitre. Perceiving below him a large corps of cavalry forming by detachments, and seeing the French cannon reopen fire, he despatched an aide-de-camp to warn the Sixty-ninth to form square, and received an answer that his orders were obeyed. The French cavalry, reinforced apparently by Lefebvre-Desnoëtte's division,[2] was in fact massing for a fourth and final attack which was to be supported by infantry. Bossu Wood had by

[1] In spite of the statements of Le Bas and Wommersom, the con-currence of testimony as to the flight of the Netherlanders at this time is so strong that I cannot overlook it. The private Journal of Colonel James Stanhope who came up with the 1st Guards says : " Soon after passing Nivelles we met a great many wounded men going to the rear with ten times their number to take care of them, which did not strike me as a good specimen of the first trial of our Allies." Such a witness had no object in saying what was untrue, and he confirms the general reports of other British writers.

[2] Or by some part of it. See Houssaye, *Waterloo*, p. 214, note. I do not see how the French cavalry could have come forward again without reinforcement : particularly as we are told that the cuirassiers took part in every one of the attacks, and only two regiments of cuirassiers were present.

this time been nearly cleared of the Allied battalions, so that Bauduin's, Jamin's and Gauthier's brigades were able to advance, some of them in the open, most of them, it should seem, within the wood itself ; and Ney had ordered two batteries of artillery to advance along a ride close to the eastern margin of the wood and running parallel with it, so as to emerge at the right moment from the wood into the plain and prepare the way for the onslaught of the infantry.

Wellington had been temporarily absent from Quatre Bras when Halkett came up, but sent an aide-de-camp to ask if Sir Colin could follow the original instructions given by Picton. He was answered that it seemed unsafe to leave the Brunswickers unsupported until more troops should come up. Halkett's brigade was therefore disposed, apparently, so as at once to take pressure off Picton's right and to maintain the defence of the north-eastern angle of the wood. The whole were echeloned,[1] it seems, to west of the Brussels road, the Sixty-ninth, together with two guns of Lloyd's battery which had just arrived, foremost, and the Thirtieth next to them. As they reached their appointed ground they began to form square, in obedience to Halkett's warning, when the Prince of Orange galloped up and asked them what they were about, as there was no fear of any further attack by cavalry. Pursuant to the Prince's command the two battalions deployed into line, and the two guns were presently recalled to join the rest of their battery just south of the farm of Quatre Bras. Cleeves's and Kuhlmann's batteries of the German Legion appeared shortly afterwards, whereupon Lloyd's took post on the west side of the road, Cleeves's on the east side, and Kuhlmann's midway between them.

Shortly afterwards the French cavalry came up the road to their fourth attack, and catching sight of

---

[1] It is most difficult to discover the position of Halkett's brigade. Amid all the libraries that have been written on the campaign of Waterloo it is almost impossible to ascertain so simple a point as this.

1815. the Thirty-third, which was moving in column of
June 16. companies through the rye on the highest point of
the plateau, galloped upon them. The battalion
formed square, whereupon the baffled horsemen,
perceiving the Sixty-ninth in a hollow below, wheeled
round and charged down upon them. The Sixty-
ninth being, through the folly of the Prince of
Orange, deployed, made shift to throw itself into
square and, apparently, would have succeeded had
not the captain of the grenadier - company wheeled
the two right-hand companies about in order to fire,
instead of closing the face of the square. In a moment
the horsemen were in the middle of them. The two
companies were destroyed, the rest were partly broken,
the only remaining colour of the battalion was captured,
one hundred and fifty men were killed and wounded,
and the remainder saved themselves by taking refuge
under the bayonets of the Forty-second and Forty-
fourth.[1] Flushed with success, the cavalry turned
upon the Thirtieth, which, however, having had time
to form square, beat them off with a steadiness which
earned warm praise from Picton. Some of the
cuirassiers then essayed a last desperate attempt upon
Quatre Bras, but were shattered to pieces by Cleeves's
guns ; and the survivors fled in headlong panic along
the Brussels road, infecting with their fright some of
the infantry as they passed, and carrying dismay even
to Charleroi and beyond.[2]

Nevertheless the danger of Wellington's situation
was never greater than at this moment. The Sixty-
ninth was for the time dispersed ; the Seventy-third,
upon the sight of the cavalry approaching them, had

[1] The Colonel, who was killed at Waterloo, told Captain Rudyard
of Lloyd's battery that the battalion was saved by the fire of a battalion
of Guards (*Waterloo Letters*, p. 231); but it is, I think, impossible
that the Guards were so early on the field.

[2] I conceive that these fugitives were the 3rd Léger of Bauduin's
brigade and possibly the 93rd Line of Gauthier's brigade. The 3rd
lost not a single officer killed or wounded, and the 93rd only two
officers.

run into the thicket;[1] and now the French batteries
concealed in the wood opened fire with deadly effect
upon the Thirty-third. After enduring the trial for
a short time the colonel deployed the battalion, and,
covered by a regiment of Brunswick cavalry, moved
towards a battalion of Brunswick infantry which was
heavily engaged in the re-entrant angle of the wood
near Quatre Bras. A cry rose that the cavalry was
again approaching, and the Thirty-third rushed into
the wood and dispersed. The Thirtieth appears to
have altered its formation and stood firm,[2] but, with
this exception, Halkett's brigade was for the time out
of action ; and the French cavalry returned to its old
task of rushing round the squares of Pack's brigade.
These still held their ground with noble tenacity, but
Bossu Wood was practically lost to the Allies for the
moment. Its eastern border was full of British troops,
but these were dispersed in the undergrowth, some
of them no doubt glad to find themselves in a safe
place and unwilling to leave it, but all, including the
officers, absolutely lost, without an idea in which
direction they were moving or ought to move, how
they were to assemble themselves and what they should
do when assembled. The French, on the other hand,
were pushing on to the Nivelles road with every
prospect of turning Wellington's right ; and, if
they should succeed in doing this, the day would be
lost.

Happily at this moment the division of Guards,
followed by two Brunswick battalions and a Brunswick battery, approached Quatre Bras, much fatigued
after a march of fifteen hours. The Prince of Orange,
in a high state of excitement, galloped out to meet
them, and encountering Lord Saltoun at the head of
the light companies of the First Guards, ordered him
to strike south-eastward into the western side of Bossu
Wood. Saltoun, unable to see any enemy, asked

---

[1] Morris. *Recollections of Military Service,* p. 197.
[2] *Life of Sir William Gomm,* p. 355.

where the French were to be found. " If you do not like to undertake it," answered the foolish Prince, excitedly, " I'll find some one who will." Saltoun, who had served with distinction through the campaigns of Coruña, Walcheren, Vitoria, the Pyrenees, and Southern France, quietly repeated his question and, upon obtaining a reasonable reply, formed his line of skirmishers and entered the wood. Guided only by the sound of the enemy's musketry, these pressed forward steadily, while the Prince of Orange, utterly ignorant of his business, hurried the succeeding companies in pairs, as they came up, close on the heels of Saltoun. Unable to see anything, these supporting companies could only fire where they could hear firing, and this undoubtedly caused some loss among Saltoun's men. However, their advance certainly checked that of the French on the western side of the wood ; and meanwhile Lloyd's battery, moving forward from Quatre Bras, engaged the two French batteries on the eastern margin of the wood. After a murderous duel which cost Lloyd several men and two complete teams, he succeeded not only in silencing them but in driving back a French column which attempted to debouch from the trees in that quarter. But farther to the north two French columns, following not far upon the heels of the defeated cuirassiers, had turned north-eastward out of the wood upon Quatre Bras, one of them occupying the house and garden of La Bergerie. Sir Edward Barnes therefore placed himself at the head of the Ninety-second, which charged the head of the leading column and drove it back into the garden. Under a murderous flanking fire from the second column the Highlanders then assaulted the building and its enclosures, cleared the enemy from it after a desperate encounter, and fairly drove the French down before them along the margin between wood and road until they came under the fire of the French guns posted on the hill opposite Gemion-court. Then at last they withdrew into the wood for shelter, whence they retired, with ranks terribly thinned, 1815. to Quatre Bras.                                                 June 16.

Not long afterwards the Second battalion of the First Guards, after not much less than an hour of confused fighting, penetrated to the extreme south-western angle of Bossu Wood, with its companies naturally much intermixed and its order in great measure lost. By that time the bulk of Halkett's brigade had been rallied and reposted level with the Gemioncourt Brook, with the two new Brunswick battalions somewhat in advance of them ; and, when the Guards emerged into the open ground, they could see the Thirty-third behind the shelter of a hedge to their left rear. They were however received by so heavy a fire of musketry and artillery when they showed themselves, that they withdrew again to a hollow formed by a rill that runs north and south through the wood, though even then they suffered some loss from heavy branches cut off by the French round-shot. Here, being joined by their Third battalion, the First Guards advanced again into the open between the wood and the Brussels road, having rallied to them a number of lost men of Halkett's brigade, while Byng's brigade came and began to form up on their right. The deployment was in process and the Brunswick battalion was moving down to form on the left of Maitland's brigade, when the French cuirassiers made a dash upon the left flank of the First Guards. The men instantly ran back to line the ditch at the edge of the wood while the Bruns-wickers formed square ; and the cuirassiers, met by the fire of the Guards in front and of the Brunswickers in flank, were driven back with very heavy loss. Never-theless all Maitland's attempts to make further progress and to storm the French battery were frustrated by the steadiness of the French infantry. On the Allied left a resolute attempt of Bachelu to turn Wellington's left was foiled, after much hard fighting, by the Rifles, with the support of two

1815.
June 16.
Hanoverian battalions ; and soon after sunset all French attacks ceased, and their cavalry vanished from the ground. Ney had, in fact, withdrawn all his troops to Frasnes; and at nine o'clock, as the darkness thickened, Wellington established his line of picquets from Petit Pierrepont, through Gemioncourt to Pireaumont, over against the outposts of Ney. Thus was recovered, after a struggle of six hours, the original position (the farm of Grand Pierrepont excepted) which had been occupied by Perponcher in the morning.

Few engagements are more difficult to follow and to understand than the battle of Quatre Bras. It is impossible, in the first place, to say definitely what numbers of the Allies were in action at any given moment after the first hour or even half-hour. Fresh troops were constantly coming up from beginning to end of the fight, and, though many authors have tried to settle the hour at which this or that brigade or division arrived on the ground, the data upon which they have reckoned are so uncertain that no reliance can be placed upon them. The hours stated by various actors who have left narratives of the struggle are, again, so contradictory that any endeavour to reconcile them is hopeless. It is also extremely hard to discover exactly what force of cavalry was at the disposal of Ney. Some narratives[1] on the side of the Allies state that Roussel's cuirassiers were present at the end of the day, but did not charge ; and indeed the ubiquity of the cuirassiers, as pourtrayed by the concurrence of many English narrators, would seem to demand the presence of more than one brigade of this particular description of cavalry. The constant mention of lancers also would seem to imply that those of Lefebvre-Desnoëttes as well as those of Piré were among the

---

[1] *E.g.* Siborne's and the French *Témoin oculaire*. See *The Battle of Waterloo, by a Near Observer* (10th ed. 1817), p. 129. Siborne also credits Ney with the whole of Héritier's cavalry division instead of with Guiton's brigade only.

squadrons which harassed Picton's battalions through 1815.
so many hours.  Yet, according to the list of casualties, June 16.
not a single officer of Roussel's brigade and only two
officers of Lefebvre-Desnoëttes's command were touched
on the 16th of June.  The height of the rye-stalks,
the veiling of the French right by Hutte Wood as of
the Allied right by Bossu Wood, and the undulations
of the ground evidently made accurate observation
impracticable.  The only certain fact that can be
adduced is that Ney began the fight with about
fifteen thousand infantry, eighteen hundred cavalry,
and thirty-eight guns against about seven thousand
infantry, with no cavalry and sixteen guns ; and that
when the battle ended Ney's force had probably been
augmented by more than a thousand horse, whereas
Wellington's had been swelled by the arrival, at
different periods, of some twenty-two thousand. men
and forty-two guns.  Of course the value of the
troops that from first to last came under Wellington's
command during the day varied very greatly, but, so
far as bare numbers go, the figures are roughly as
above stated.  That Wellington was in constant peril
was due to the facts, first, that every successive reinforcement as it came up had to bear the full weight
of the French attack, which had already overwhelmed
its predecessors ; and secondly, that he had no British
cavalry present.  For these disadvantages no one can
be held responsible but himself.

The conduct of the troops of all nations in the field,
without exception, varied greatly.  Taking first the
Netherlanders, to whom without dispute belongs the
credit of occupying and defending the position of
Quatre Bras in the first instance, it appears that the
27th Chasseurs, the 5th Militia and the 2nd Nassau
Light Infantry, all three of them, lost heavily in killed
and wounded ; but of the wounded a very large proportion were but slightly hurt, and the 27th and the
5th both show a discreditable number of men missing.
The losses of the seven remaining battalions, so far as

1815.
June 16.

they are returned, were slight—indeed, except in one instance, so trifling as to prove that those units took only a minute share in the action.[1]   On the other hand, Van Merlen's two cavalry regiments seem to have behaved better, though here again the proportion of slightly wounded is unduly large ;  and Stevenaart's battery of artillery, which lost all its officers and fifty killed or wounded,[2] must have behaved not only well but heroically.   The casualties of the Netherlanders, all told, amounted to a thousand and fifty-eight, of which nearly three hundred were missing and nearly four hundred slightly wounded, leaving a balance of only four to five hundred killed or seriously hurt.  For a total force of nine thousand present, most of them for the entire day, such a tale of casualties does not suggest very strenuous resistance or very serious loss ;  and, in spite of all that has been written in defence of their countrymen by Netherlandish authors, the contemporary judgment which threw the brunt of the day's work upon the British and Germans must stand as confirmed.   Nevertheless it would be unfair to judge too harshly troops so lately raised for a sovereign so newly appointed ;  and at all events the highest praise must be given to the Netherlandish Generals, Constant and Perponcher.  The like cannot be said of the Prince of Orange, who succeeded in destroying one British battalion, and did his best to destroy three more. His courage was unquestionable, but, considered as a general officer, he can be described only as a meddlesome and mischievous encumbrance.

Of the Brunswickers, those that were rallied by Halkett were not seen at their best, but the rest appear

---

[1] One battalion of militia is omitted from the return altogether, which, unless it were dissolved, is rather remarkable.

[2] The figure given by Le Bas and Wommersom in their text (i. 507) is 1 officer and 28 men killed, 2 officers and 83 men wounded, making 114 casualties out of 119 present.  This does not agree with the return printed in vol. iii. 201, where the figures are 1 officer and 6 men killed, 2 officers and 13 men severely wounded, 3 officers and 25 men slightly wounded, 14 men missing.  Total casualties 63.

to have conducted themselves well, indeed, for young soldiers, admirably. Their losses amounted to nearly eight hundred and fifty, one quarter of them missing ; two battalions having each about one hundred casualties and a third close upon two hundred. The Hanoverians also displayed commendable steadiness in spite of the misfortune which overtook one of their battalions. Their casualties well exceeded six hundred. Of the British the battalions of Picton's division rose to the highest level of excellence attained by British infantry, their constancy under repeated devastation by artillery and incessant attacks of cavalry being superb. The Guards also maintained worthily their high reputation, being thrown into action at a very trying moment after a march of twenty-six miles, with shaken troops on every side of them. The casualties among them and the battalions of Picton's division were heavy. In the First Guards the Second and Third battalions lost over five hundred out of two thousand rank and file. In Pack's brigade, the Royals had over two hundred killed and wounded, and Forty-second and Ninety-second each over two hundred and eighty, representing in the case of the two last not far from one - half of their numbers. In Kempt's brigade the Thirty-second had very nearly two hundred casualties, and the Seventy-ninth just over three hundred. Halkett's brigade, excepting the Sixty-ninth, escaped more lightly ; but it must be frankly confessed that as a body they behaved ill, though Halkett himself selected only the Thirty-third for reproach. But they were raw young soldiers, remnants of Graham's force, and were hardly equal to the severe trial of remaining stationary under the fire of cannon, varied only by occasional charges of cavalry ; and the Prince of Orange's disastrous interference with their formation was not calculated to inspire them with confidence. Nevertheless, their behaviour was a blot upon the general conduct of the red-coats. The total losses of the British amounted to close upon twenty-three hundred, among whom the missing did not amount to forty. The casualties of the entire force of the Allies reached the total of forty-eight hundred exactly.

The losses of the French are stated at forty-one to forty-two hundred, which is probably not far from correct. The distribution of loss, so far as can be gathered from the only ·source of information—the casualty-list of officers—was almost startlingly unequal. In Bachelu's division there fell altogether thirty-six officers, of whom fourteen belonged to the 61st of the Line, five to the 72nd, and seventeen to the 108th. On the whole this division suffered severely. In Jerome's division, the number was the same, thirty-six, but of these twenty-seven belonged to the 1st of the Line and six to the 2nd, while in Bauduin's brigade only three officers were killed or wounded in the 1st Light and not one in the 3rd Light. From this it is tolerably certain that Bauduin's brigade was but slightly engaged, and that the 3rd Light ran away in the panic caused by the flight of the cuirassiers. In Foy's division eight officers only fell in Gauthier's brigade, whereas in Jamin's no fewer than twenty-nine were killed and wounded in the 4th Light alone, besides fifteen of the 100th of the Line. Foy states his losses at seven to eight hundred, but it is manifest that the brunt fell on one regiment principally ; and, when one reflects on the small share of the work which was evidently done by Bauduin, one cannot but be filled with admiration for the persistent gallantry of the remainder of the French infantry and in particular of the 1st Line and the 4th Light. Not all the endeavours of the Guards could avail to recover more ground than had been held by the Netherlanders in the morning ; and this is no small tribute to the tenacity of their enemies. Not less remarkable was the inexhaustible courage and energy of Piré's lancers and of Guiton's cuirassiers, who suffered terribly in their attacks upon the British infantry. Here, however, there is again an irregularity in the distribution of the casualties which is difficult to explain. The 5th Lancers lost ten officers, the 6th eleven ; but the 1st Chasseurs of the same division lost only two and the 6th Chasseurs not one. In Guiton's brigade there fell of the 8th Cuirassiers alone thirteen officers, but of the 11th Cuirassiers only four. Lastly, in Lefebvre-Desnoëttes' division two officers of the Lancers of the Guard were wounded, but not one of the Chasseurs. The conclusion would seem to be that Ney at no time threw the whole of his forces into the fight, which is one more testimony to the bravery and endeavour of those that were actually engaged.

A great deal has been written, after the event, of Ney's shortcomings in the morning of the 16th, his failure to assemble his infantry betimes at Quatre Bras, and his omission to ascertain the strength of the Allies by a reconnaissance in force. Such criticism is easy, but it takes no account of the false view of the entire situation which had been held up to the Marshal by his master Napoleon. Setting aside his unsurpassable moral and physical courage, Ney had never been much more than an exceedingly skilful tactician in the field, being content with his chief's direction in higher matters. He had only joined the army after the actual opening of the campaign, consequently he knew nothing about his command, and little more than had been vouchsafed to him in Napoleon's first letter about the plan of operations. The Emperor had given him plainly to understand that the road to Brussels was open, and probably the road to Gembloux also. Ney naturally presumed that his chief knew best, and he no doubt laid himself out for a quiet day in which to settle down to his work before the march to Brussels at nightfall. Napoleon had in fact fallen into the error which he had so frequently rebuked in his subordinates—*il se faisait des tableaux*, he had conjured up imaginary pictures of the situation. He had made up his mind that both of the Allied armies were retreating, when he discovered first that the Prussians were standing firm and ready to accept battle. For this he was more or less prepared. He had his two wings and his reserve ready for such a contingency, and welcomed the opportunity of annihilating one army while in isolation from the other. Once again he conjured up a picture of forty thousand Prussians only before him, whereas there proved to be eighty thousand. For this also he was in a measure ready, for he had announced that, when necessary, he should weaken one wing to strengthen the other. He accordingly proceeded first to summon Ney's entire force to him, and meanwhile took d'Erlon's corps from him bodily. But, as the proceedings of the day developed, it became apparent that the French army was saddled, not with one pitched battle, but with two. Both wings were busily engaged at one and the same time, which was contrary to all of Napoleon's principles and plans, and the reserve was reduced practically to d'Erlon's corps, which was needed and clamoured for equally by Napoleon and by Ney.

The not unnatural result was that d'Erlon spent the day marching backwards and forwards between Ligny and Quatre Bras, and did not finally settle down at Frasnes until night had put an end to the fighting everywhere. His corps thrown in upon either battle-field would undoubtedly have secured a decided success for the Emperor; and d'Erlon has been much blamed for obeying Ney's command to return from St. Amand. We have seen enough of this officer during the campaign in the Pyrenees to know that he was not a man to commit himself upon any side so long as he could find a safe way in the middle; and it is therefore not surprising that he should have acted as he did. But the key to his irresolution and to Ney's apathy was undoubtedly Napoleon's misjudgment of the whole situation. Napoleon's first word on the 16th was, practically, " There will be no fighting to-day "; his second, " I shall fight a battle to-day, and shall need all my reserves to make it decisive " ; whereas events proved that he was destined to fight two severe battles, one of them successful, the other unsuccessful, but neither decisive. A little more tactical skill on the part of Blücher would have made both of them unsuccessful, and then his plan of campaign would have been ruined. Even as it was, his losses—certainly not far short of thirteen thousand men—incurred as they were for no final result, threatened to work havoc with his operations, for it was certain that two more such engagements would bring his army to a standstill. Altogether the 16th of June was a bad day for Napoleon, and chiefly through his own fault. The fact is that he overrated the effect of his prestige, and omitted from his calculations the important factor that the two generals opposed to him were not afraid of him. Still less did he bethink him that one of the two was a commander whom his own generals were afraid to meet. But for the unpleasant memories of Peninsular battles Ney would probably have attacked earlier, and taken Quatre Bras before Picton's division could have arrived in time to save it. The events of the 16th of June turned, it may be said, chiefly on the singular circumstance that, at any rate for that day, Wellington's name inspired greater awe into the French than Napoleon's into the Allies.

# CHAPTER IV

1815.  THE armies of Napoleon, Wellington and Ney were
June 16. all of them too much exhausted to move on the evening
of the 16th; but the Prussians had no choice but to
retire.  Some of their Ist and IInd Corps had been
very severely handled and were to some extent de-
moralised.  Fugitives swarmed along the road to
Liége, and, though many were turned back by Prussian officers, it was reckoned that from eight to ten
thousand forsook their colours and pursued their way
in no sort of order.  Some hundreds of Prussian
marauders and bad characters, indeed, even found
their way to Brussels, where, among other depreda-
tions, they stole several horses belonging to British
officers.[1]  On the other hand, the actual losses in
action did not exceed six thousand, of which only a
small proportion were prisoners, and the guns captured by the French little exceeded twenty.  Two
of Ziethen's brigades and one of Thielmann's had
firmly arrested the French advances at Brye and before
Sombreffe ;  and Thielmann, whose corps had been
little engaged, finally stood fast about Sombreffe till
past ten o'clock.  Gneisenau, who was left in command owing to Blücher's injuries, had at first given
provisional orders for retreat northward to Tilly ;  but
he was much inclined to fall back upon Liége, and it
was only after a warm discussion between him,
Blücher and Grolmann that he at last gave way to
them, and early in the morning of the 17th issued the

1 Jackson. *Notes and Reminiscences of a Staff Officer*, pp. 35-36.

final command for retreat to Wavre. This decision has been rightly styled the turning point of the campaign, and, so far as Blücher and Grolmann were concerned, it certainly signified their fixed intention to stand by their Allies. Gneisenau was influenced by no such motive ; and indeed the movement by no means necessarily bound him to co-operation with Wellington. A retreat upon Liége, if carried out by the Roman road, would not have been the safest of operations with a Napoleon within striking distance, whereas by retiring northward to Louvain he could strike a second and far securer line of communication with the Rhine Provinces by Maastricht and Aix-la-Chapelle. Head-quarters for the night were fixed at Mellery, and at daybreak of the 17th the whole army marched upon Wavre, where Pirch I.'s corps took up its bivouac to south at Ste. Anne and Aisemont, Ziethen's to west at Bierges, and Thielmann's to north at La Bavette. Bülow at the same time was called in to Dion-le-Mont, about three miles south-east of Wavre, where he arrived at ten o'clock at night. Thus the Prussian army effected its retirement without molestation, and on the night of the 17th was concentrated in full force and by no means in bad heart. The only thing which the Prussian staff had omitted to do was to inform Wellington of their retreat.

At Quatre Bras the British cavalry continued to stream in through the evening and night; and by daybreak of the 17th all six of the brigades, one regiment excepted, had arrived, bringing the total of the force up to forty-five thousand men. Two aides-de-camp had been sent to Wellington by Gneisenau in the course of the 16th, the first of whom was wounded near Pireaumont and never delivered his message, while the second brought the news that, though no great success was to be expected as the outcome of the fight, the Prussians hoped to hold their ground till nightfall. Relying upon this assurance the Duke rested at Genappe for the night, returning to Quatre Bras soon after

1815. daylight. There was some firing among the most
June 17. advanced skirmishers upon both sides, which after a
time died away. As there was still no information
from the Prussians and it was therefore uncertain
whether the next march was to be in advance or in
retreat, Wellington soon after six o'clock sent a staff
officer, Sir Alexander Gordon, escorted by a troop of the
Tenth Hussars, towards Ligny. This party, after
driving in a French picquet about Marbais, turned north
and, meeting General Ziethen, who was directing the
movements of the Prussian rear-guard, ascertained from
him the truth respecting the events of the 16th.
When Gordon returned with his report, the Duke
looked meaningly at Müffling, who, conscious of his
own good faith, explained that the Prussian aide-de-
camp, who had been wounded at Pireaumont, had
probably been sent to convey this very news. Wellington, instantly pacified, proceeded to discuss what
should be done. At present he knew only that
Blücher had retreated upon Wavre and that Bülow's
corps had not been engaged ; and the only course
appeared to be to retire to some position level with
Wavre, and to regulate his future operations by the
reports that should reach him from Blücher. After
some hesitation the Duke decided to let the men cook
and eat their breakfasts before moving ; and at nine
o'clock a Prussian officer arrived to report Blücher's
resolution of concentrating at Wavre, and to ascertain
Wellington's intentions. The Duke answered that he
should retire to Mont St. Jean, where, if supported by
one Prussian corps, he should accept battle.

The retreat of Pirch I. and Ziethen, astonishing to
say, was unobserved on the French left ; but on the
right Pajol's patrols reported at half-past two in the
morning that the Prussians were in motion, and Pajol
without delay sent two regiments in pursuit along
the road to Namur. Stragglers and lost units, including a stray squadron and a stray battery, induced the
French hussars to follow this false track, and at five

o'clock Pajol reported definitely that the enemy was 1815.
retreating along the road to Namur and Liége. June 17.
Pursuing his way for some hours, however, he began
to doubt if he were right, and at noon, upon the information of some peasants, he turned northwards by
a by-road towards Louvain.    Berton's brigade of Exelmans's cavalry corps also followed the road to Namur
for a short distance, but soon turned towards Gembloux, where at nine o'clock in the morning it came
upon Thielmann's whole corps halted for rest.    Exelmans himself presently came up, but contented himself
with watching the Prussians and sending a despatch,
rather late, to report that he was doing so.

Meanwhile, at about seven o'clock, the Emperor
received Pajol's message above mentioned ; and nearly
at the same time his aide-de-camp, Flahault, returned
from Quatre Bras and gave an account of what had
passed there.    Deciding not to issue any definite orders,
Napoleon gave Ney notice that he was proceeding
to Brye, and that, if there were any trouble with the
British army, he would attack it in flank while Ney
assailed it in front, so as to compel it to yield up
Quatre Bras.    The rest of the day, he added, would
be spent in collecting stragglers and replenishing stores.
At nine o'clock, accordingly, he left Fleurus for the
battle-field of Ligny, where he inspected his troops and
visited the wounded.    Here letters reached him from
Ney, from Pajol and from Exelmans.    The first set
forth that the Allied troops at Quatre Bras were an
army and not a mere rear-guard ; the second reported
the capture of guns and prisoners at Mazy on the
Namur road ; and the third announced that Exelmans
was marching with his cavalry corps upon Gembloux in pursuit of the Prussians.[1]    Thereupon
Napoleon decided to divide his army, and delivered his

[1] Houssaye : *Waterloo*, p. 232.    I think it too much to assume,
as Houssaye does, that Exelmans's first report announced that the
Prussians were at Gembloux in force.    This first report does not exist
and can only be reconstructed, by implication, from the text of a second
report, which, in my opinion, warrants no such construction.

1815. final instructions to that end.   To Grouchy he handed
June 17. over Teste's division of Lobau's corps, Vandamme's
and Gérard's corps complete, and the four cavalry
divisions of Pajol and Exelmans, with instructions to
proceed with them to Gembloux.   From that centre
the Marshal was to explore in the direction of Namur
and Maastricht, pursue the enemy and discover his
movements.   Napoleon himself would meanwhile proceed to Quatre Bras ; and the line of communications,
which was to be well guarded, would be by the paved
road to Namur.   In any case, Grouchy was to keep
his infantry in a compact body with several avenues of
retreat.   " It is important," so ran one sentence, " to
discover what Blücher and Wellington mean to do,
and whether they intend to unite their armies to cover
Brussels and Liége by trying their luck in another
battle." [1]

According to the purport of these instructions, as
I read them, Grouchy's mission was to be one principally of reconnaissance and exploration.   The Emperor
repeats twice in the course of a few lines that he wishes
to penetrate his enemy's intentions.   With this object,
chiefly, as the text appears to indicate, Grouchy was
to pursue the Prussians, and, though he was to start
at Gembloux, he was directed particularly to make
good the ground towards Namur, and indeed to cause
that line to be occupied by National Guards in case
it had been evacuated by the Prussians.   This shows
plainly that Napoleon was still wedded to his original
idea, confirmed as it was to some extent by Pajol's
reports, that Blücher had retreated eastwards.   In
this case Grouchy might have to deal with a strong
rear-guard at Gembloux ; and it was, apparently, to

[1] There are various readings of this order, in some of which the
words " or Liége " are omitted.   In yet another version the sentence
runs, " It is important to discover what the Prussians mean to do ;
either they are separating themselves from the English or intend
to try their luck in another battle."   I follow the text given by
Houssaye, pp. 236, 237, which is drawn from the Archives de la
Guerre at Paris.

meet this contingency that he had been entrusted with
a force of over thirty thousand men. Further, Napoleon
evidently contemplated the chance of his meeting with
the entire Prussian army, or at any rate with a
superior force, otherwise he would not have added
the admonition that many avenues of retreat should
be kept open for the infantry.    The possibility that
Wellington and Blücher might unite their armies and
fight a battle to cover Brussels and Liége is treated
in extremely obscure language.    The only line on
which a single battle could be fought to cover both
places would be that of the previous day, Quatre Bras
and Sombreffe, or perhaps Quatre Bras and Gembloux.
Did Napoleon expect Wellington and Blücher each of
them to assemble his whole army (which so far neither
of them had done) and to fight another action at
Quatre Bras and Gembloux, at which points the pair
of them were said to be massed in strength ?    It must
be presumed that he did, for, if the two were to fight
united in a single array, they could only do so safely
by converging north-west and north-east ; and not a
word was said to Grouchy about exploring at all in a
northerly direction or west of Gembloux.

Such vagueness of instruction can only be engendered
by uncertainty and confusion of thought.    What Napoleon expected and hoped was that the main body of
the Prussians was already withdrawing to Liége by way
of Tongres and Namur, and that Grouchy would break
down their rear-guard and drive it in the same
direction, following it up and keeping it at a distance,
while the Emperor himself should fall upon the British.
He gave special injunctions that frequent intelligence
should be sent to him in case he should be mistaken ;
but he did not give Grouchy to understand that the
right wing was to act as right-flank-guard to the left
wing and reserve, while the Emperor dealt with the
British army.    It is true that a commander cannot
always reveal to a subordinate all that is in his mind :
that must depend on various considerations, personal

and other.   If Napoleon had manifested his true meaning to Grouchy, the latter might have asked how he was to fend off ninety thousand men with thirty thousand ; and the question would have been an extremely awkward one.   Yet, as it seems to me, this is the gist of the whole matter, that Grouchy did not know what his master wanted, because his master either did not know or dared not tell him.   The truth is that the result of the two actions on the 16th amounted to a defeat for Napoleon, and left him not indeed without resource—his genius was too great for that—but with insuperable difficulties before him.

Meanwhile at nine o'clock Wellington had issued his orders for retreat.   The Second British Division, part of the Fourth British Division and the Third Netherlandish Division were to march to Waterloo from Nivelles, and the Second Netherlandish Division from Quatre Bras, at once.   The remainder of the Fourth Division was to halt at Braine-le-Comte.   The rest of the infantry was to assemble to right and left of the position, holding its former ground only with its picquets, and at one o'clock the cavalry was to form in rear of the position in three lines to cover the march of the infantry.   The corps of Prince Frederick of Orange was to retire from Enghien to Hal in the evening, and the Fourth Division (less Mitchell's brigade) was to move likewise to Hal in the morning of the 18th.

The movement, screened by all the skill of which Wellington was master, began before ten o'clock, and continued quietly, though the Duke watched the front with anxiety until the last of the battalions marched off, when he said, " Well, there is the last of the infantry gone, and I don't care now."   Ney throughout this time remained perfectly inactive, which was, in the circumstances, not surprising.   He had been placed in a false position on the 16th ; he had suffered heavy loss for no commensurate object in consequence ; he had been left all night unaware of the issue of the battle of Ligny ; and, of the letters received by him from Napoleon's head-quarters on the 17th, one expressed displeasure and reproach for the isolation of d'Erlon's corps, while the other held out the prospect of a quiet day to be devoted to re-equipment and to the replenishment of stores.   To this it must be added that the discipline of the French army was extremely bad, and that the soldiers had fallen at once into the evil ways, taught to them by many campaigns, of marauding and plunder.   Even the Emperor's maga-zines had not been spared, and the Guard had been among the worst offenders.   The Provost Marshal, in fact, resigned his appointment on the 17th in despair over his impotence to set matters right.[1]   After a hard and discouraging day's fighting in weather of intense heat, the men had probably indemnified them-selves by dispersing during the night in search of such luxuries as were to be obtained by pillage ;  and it is reasonable to suppose that, until late in the forenoon, the ranks of many regiments were much depleted. However that may be, there was up to one o'clock no sign of life on the French side at Quatre Bras ; and Napoleon, who had arrived at about that hour at Marbais, losing patience made his way thither in person with Lobau's corps, the Guard, Domont's and Subervie's divisions of light cavalry and Milhaud's division of cuirassiers.   His advanced parties struck against those of the British cavalry shortly afterwards, whereupon Napoleon deployed his force into two lines, the cavalry in front with the artillery massed in the centre, and the infantry in rear, and sent a message to Ney to advance immediately.

Wellington had for some hours past taken up his station close to Quatre Bras, sometimes seated on the ground reading and laughing over the English news-papers, sometimes riding a short distance forward to sweep the ground with his telescope.   He was much astonished that the enemy made no movement, and

[1] Houssaye, *Waterloo*, p. 80.

1815.
June 17. seemed to think it within the bounds of possibility that they might have retreated. The air was intensely hot and oppressively still. Angry thunderclouds were heaping themselves up to northward ; and altogether it was such a day as saps human energy and makes even the most active man hope inwardly for peace and quiet. Wellington was undeceived by the sight of a mass of cuirsasiers forming alongside the Namur road about two miles away—evidently the first step in Napoleon's manœuvre of deployment. At about two o'clock the cuirassiers were observed to mount and to ride forward, preceded by lancers ; the advanced parties of the British horse both in the front and on the left flank became engaged ; and presently a picquet of the Eighteenth Hussars came trotting in, without loss, along the Namur road. Wellington then left the conduct of the retreat to Lord Uxbridge, giving orders that anything like a serious engagement must, if possible, be avoided. Uxbridge accordingly directed the retirement to be made in three columns. The two heavy brigades of Somerset and Ponsonby, together with the Seventh Hussars and Twenty-third Light Dragoons, formed the centre, which was to take the Brussels road ; Vandeleur's and Vivian's brigades composed the left or eastern column, which was to move by Baisy and Thy ; Dörnberg's brigade and the Fifteenth Hussars made up the right column, which was to pass the Thy rivulet above Genappe. Vivian's brigade, being on the extreme left, was drawn up in line at right angles to the Namur road, with its left thrown back and two guns upon the road itself.

As the French cavalry advanced, the British cannon opened fire ; and then, whether owing to the concussion or not, the storm-cloud burst with a blinding flash and a terrific roar, while the rain poured down in such streams as are rarely seen even within the tropics.[1] Vivian, however, had already observed the French horse turning

[1] All accounts agree that the storm was of exceptional violence, and the rain extraordinarily heavy.

northward to outflank him ; so, ordering his battery to
retire with all speed, he put his brigade about[1] and
fell back upon Vandeleur's brigade, half a mile in
rear. Vandeleur, instead of waiting for Vivian's
brigade to pass through his own, withdrew as Vivian
approached him, wherein he was probably right,
though Vivian was of a different opinion.[2] The
incident showed the danger of allowing brigades to
manœuvre on their own account without the control
of a divisional commander. The French were riding
fast to come up on Vivian's left and envelop him,
but the ground had become so deep under the deluge
of rain that their pace failed, and Vivian was able to
gain the bridge over the Thy with little loss. The
fire of a few dismounted men sufficed to check further
pursuit by the French when they reached the bridge
itself ; and the brigade reached its bivouac with
trifling loss.

In the centre Somerset's and Ponsonby's brigades
passed through Genappe, which was the only serious
defile in the road, without difficulty, and formed at
the summit of a gentle slope on the north side of the
village, having the Twenty-third Light Dragoons a
little in advance of them, while the Seventh Hussars
as rear-guard remained on the southern side. Though
the bridge at Genappe was so narrow as to admit
horsemen only in single file, the Seventh was withdrawn safely across it with no great difficulty and was
formed in front of the Twenty-third, with one squadron
in advance. A quarter of an hour later the French
1st Lancers debouched from Genappe, preceded by a
small party of headlong troopers who proved, when
captured, to be drunk. In the narrow streets of the
village the columns became so much crowded that
Uxbridge ordered a squadron of the Seventh Hussars

---

[1] " There began at the same moment as we went threes about
a shower of rain, the heaviest I ever experienced." Memoirs of the
18th Hussars, p. 139. (I have altered the original spelling of the
writer, the adjutant of the 18th, who rose from the ranks.)

[2] Tomkinson, p. 284 : Waterloo Letters, pp. 155-156.

to charge.   They did so, but, though received at the
halt by the enemy, were unable to make any impression
upon the narrow front of lances which met them in
the streets.   After a confused struggle of cutting and
thrusting with alternations of success and failure on
both sides, the Seventh were finally repulsed, and the
lancers imprudently following them up the hill in
pursuit were charged by two squadrons of the First
Life Guards.   Under the weight of big men on big
horses the lancers were borne back in confusion into
the village, where, crushed together in the narrow
streets, they could not use their lances and as a natural
result were very roughly handled.

The retreat was then recommenced, covered by the
Union Brigade ; but the pursuit was little pressed, for
the ground, except on the paved road, was everywhere
fetlock-deep and in the ploughed fields hock-deep, so
much so that Uxbridge gradually drew the whole of his
men to the road.   By evening the whole had reached
Wellington's chosen position on the ridge of Mont St.
Jean.   As usual, Wellington had hidden his troops
away on the reverse slope ; and Napoleon, at the head
of his advanced cavalry, could see little when the head
of his column came up to the ale-house called La
Belle Alliance, which stands on the eastern side of the
Brussels road about fourteen hundred yards south of
the centre of Wellington's position.   The Emperor
therefore unlimbered four batteries, two of which
opened fire, and deployed his cuirassiers as if for
attack.   The challenge, to Wellington's great annoy-
ance, was at once taken up by Cleeves's and Lloyd's
batteries, which opened upon the columns of French
infantry whose heads had begun to show themselves
about La Belle Alliance.   The Duke presently ordered
these guns to cease fire, and Napoleon withdrew,
having ascertained what he wanted to know, that the
Allies were present in force.

French authors have called the retreat from Quatre
Bras to Waterloo a disorderly movement, and one has

gone so far as to call the French advance upon the
heels of the Allies " a furious pursuit." It does
indeed appear that Uxbridge, perhaps ambitious of
distinction, delayed the withdrawal of the cavalry for
longer than was necessary or prudent, and that for a
time the retreat of a part of it was, by Uxbridge's
order and example, extremely hurried. Gardiner's
battery of horse artillery, according to one of its
subalterns, galloped for nearly the whole of the
distance, and Mercer's was also hustled backward
in the same fashion. This haste seems, however, to
have been urged upon the artillery only, in order to
get them out of the way ; and, even so, time was
found to replace the cast shoe of a gun-horse of
Gardiner's battery, which does not point to great
pressure on the part of the pursuers. The casualty-
lists likewise fail to bear out the French contention.
The total losses of the cavalry on the 17th amounted
to ninety-three killed, wounded and missing, of whom
forty-six belonged to the Seventh Hussars and eighteen
to the Life-Guards, which were the only corps seriously
engaged. The twenty-nine remaining casualties were
distributed among seven different regiments, and
were evidently due to the fire of artillery. A pursuit
which produced no greater results could not have been
very furious. Possibly, but for the heavy rain, the
French might have pressed the British horse more
severely ; but even this is doubtful. The only time
at which the French threatened any formidable
enveloping movement was before the Allied rear-
guard had reached Genappe ; and the soil was not at
that period so much saturated as to impede their
movements seriously. Yet they accomplished nothing;
and Vivian's brigade, which was at one moment that
which was in greatest danger, escaped with five
casualties. Altogether Uxbridge's account of the
affair is probably correct—that it was the prettiest
field-day of cavalry and horse-artillery that he ever
witnessed.

1815.   Throughout the afternoon and evening the rain
June 17. continued with little intermission, and after nightfall
it seems to have gathered new vigour and to have
poured down steadily.   Every soul in both armies
was soaked to the skin.   The tall rye, which covered
most of the ground, was like standing water, and the
ground was soon poached into mud knee-deep.   It
was difficult to light fires and impossible to keep them
up.   The Allies were better off than their opponents,
for some at least of them had reached their bivouacs
while the ground was still dry ; and there was food
for them when they arrived.   The French infantry,
on the other hand, did not come to their halting place
until after dark, in some cases not until far into the
night, after a most exhausting march through the mud ;
and the service of supply was, as usual, defective.   All
discipline seems to have ceased for the time.   The
men dispersed in search of food and shelter, pillaging
mercilessly in all directions ;  and many of the cavalry
remounted their horses and slept all night in the saddle
as the best means of keeping dry,[1] a fact which is not
without its bearing on the events of the next day.
Napoleon himself indicated the stations for the corps
that came up with him.   D'Erlon's corps and Jacquinot's cavalry were foremost about Plancenoit,
about half a mile in rear of La Belle Alliance, and the
cavalry of Milhaud, Domont, Subervie and of the
Guard immediately to rear of them.   Reille, Lobau
and Kellermann's Cuirassiers stopped at Genappe.
The infantry of the Guard, vainly striving to reach
head-quarters, for the most part lost their way and
sought shelter where they could for the night ; two
or three regiments alone arriving towards midnight
at Glabais, two miles south of Plancenoit.   The
Emperor himself slept at Le Caillou, about a mile

[1] If this were not narrated by a French authority (Houssaye, p.
274) I should hesitate to believe it.   The French had a bad reputation
as horse-masters throughout the Napoleonic wars, but this is the worst
example of the defect that I have encountered.

and a half south of La Belle Alliance on the Brussels
road.

While the French left wing and reserve were thus
engaged, Grouchy had set the right wing in march
for Gembloux, bidding Gérard's corps halt while
Vandamme's marched past it to take the head of the
column. Vandamme moved slowly, not reaching Point
du Jour, where the road from Ligny to Gembloux
crosses that from Quatre Bras to Namur, until three
o'clock. Arriving there at about the same time
Grouchy found news from Exelmans that the Prussian
army was massed on the Orneau, and that he should
follow it as soon as it moved. Exelmans, however,
allowed Thielmann's corps (for it was that which he
had under observation) to slip away unnoticed ; and,
when the infantry marched into Gembloux between
six and seven o'clock, much harassed by bad roads
and rain, Grouchy decided to halt them there for the
night.

The messages sent in by his cavalry in the evening
indicated that the Prussian column, which had seemed
to be marching on Namur, was really moving upon
Louvain ; and intelligence from peasants, confirmed
by the reports of the French light horse which arrived
in the course of the night, went to show that the retreating enemy was moving towards Wavre. Putting
all his information together, Grouchy reported to
Napoleon at ten o'clock that the Prussian army had
parted into three columns, of which one had retired on
Namur, a second, which he supposed to be Blücher's,
was withdrawing by the Roman road towards Liége,
and a third was on its way to Wavre, presumably with
the object of joining Wellington. He added that he
was sending cavalry out towards the Roman road and
should act according to their intelligence, following
the principal mass of the Prussians in whatever direction they might take, whether to Perwez on the east
or to Wavre on the north, to prevent them in this
latter case from reaching Brussels and to separate them

from Wellington.   But, in the orders which he issued for the morrow, he directed every part of his force to the east, evidently expecting to find the mass of the Prussians in that quarter.   He seems to have regarded it as a small matter that perhaps a single corps of Blücher's army might be on its way to join Wellington.   His business was to recover and to maintain contact with the main body, wherever it might be. The Prussians were assumed to have been badly beaten ;  and, if one column of them had turned east, towards their base, and another north, presumably (though it was by no means certain) to gain Brussels, it was most probable that the main body would wheel eastward also.   So Grouchy appears to have reasoned ; nor, saving the false assumption in regard to the Prussians, which was Napoleon's and not his own, did he reason unintelligently.   His force was strong enough to press a defeated enemy in retreat, but not to combat an advancing enemy of thrice his strength.

Blücher, for his part, on the night of the 17th issued his orders in loyal fulfilment of his promise to Wellington.   Bülow's corps was directed to march at daybreak to Chapelle St. Lambert, about four miles due east of Mont St. Jean, and Pirch I.'s to follow him to the same place.   Arrived there, they were to halt and keep themselves concealed if the Allies were not seriously engaged, but, in the contrary event, they were to advance and fall upon Napoleon's right or eastern flank.   Thielmann's and Ziethen's corps were to remain on the Dyle until the movements and intentions of the French at Gembloux—Grouchy's troops —should become clearer ;  but Blücher hoped to lead them also to the assistance of the British.   This determination was taken by Blücher against the advice of Gneisenau, and, as a broad principle of action, conceded all that Wellington could have wished.   But the details of execution left much to be desired. Ziethen's corps at Bierges was within four miles of Chapelle St. Lambert as the crow flies, Thielmann's at La Bavette within five miles, Pirch I.'s at Aisemont 1815. within six miles, and Bülow's at Dion-le-Mont within June 17. seven miles. Thus, when every hour of time was precious, it was the corps remotest from Wellington which was selected to march to his aid. There was one very good reason for choosing Bülow's corps in preference to Ziethen's for this service, because Bülow's, though much harassed by long marches, had not yet been engaged, whereas Ziethen's had lost heavily both on the 15th and the 16th ; but there was no such excuse to be alleged for detaining Thielmann's corps, which had not suffered severely at Ligny. Moreover, even granting that the preference of Bülow's and Pirch I.'s corps were correct, the arrangements made for their march were, to say the least, defective. Bülow was directed not only to lead the way but to defile through the narrow streets of Wavre, whereby not merely was his journey prolonged by two miles, but the whole of Pirch's troops were compelled to mark time until the IVth Corps had passed on before them. If the Prussian staff, with Gneisenau at its head, did not foresee these complications and their inevitable result, it stands convicted of gross incompetence ; if it did foresee them, and of deliberate design contrived them, it cannot be acquitted of despicable disloyalty to the Allies of Prussia and to the common cause of Europe.

Events at the Prussian head-quarters in the early June 18. morning of the 18th throw further light upon the proceedings of the Staff. Pirch I.'s corps was under arms at five o'clock, but Bülow's leading division did not reach Wavre until seven. Had all gone well— and it will be seen presently that all did not go well —Bülow's corps could not have cleared the village and the passages of the Dyle before ten o'clock, so that at best Pirch I.'s corps must have lost three or four hours' rest for no object whatever. The consequences to the advance of a third corps in the same direction were still more serious. Before eight o'clock a

Prussian staff-officer came in from the outposts and
reported that the French at Gembloux had not moved,
but appeared not to exceed fifteen thousand. " But,"
he added, " if they should be thirty thousand, one
corps will be sufficient to guard the line of the Dyle,
for the real issue of the campaign will be decided at
Mont St. Jean." Blücher, quite agreeing with this
view, wrote to Müffling at half-past nine that he should
lead his troops in person to attack the French right
wing, as soon as Napoleon should make any movement
against Wellington ; and he proposed, if Napoleon
should not attack on the 18th, that the British and
Prussians united should attack the Emperor on the
19th. The Field-marshal, beyond all dispute, was
staunch enough, but not so Gneisenau. Of his own
motive and without consultation with his chief, he
added to this letter a postscript, begging Müffling to
make quite sure that Wellington really intended to
fight at Mont St. Jean, and not merely to make a
demonstration, which might be fatal to the Prussian
army. " It is of the highest importance "—such
were the closing words—" to know exactly what the
Duke will do, in order to arrange our movements."
Here we see Gneisenau naked and unashamed.
Wellington had declared his intention to fight if
Blücher would support him. Blücher had accepted
the declaration, as made, with all possible good faith,
and promised the assistance for which Wellington
asked. And then Gneisenau intervened, with dark
hints that Wellington designed only to entrap the
Prussian army so as to save his own, and that Blücher's
promise (for such is the purport of the words quoted
above) must after all depend upon fresh assurances from
Müffling. No intellectual eminence can exalt a nature
so essentially low as this, a nature which, from sheer
terror of that which is high, abases all others to its
own vile and despicable level. It was no fault of
Gneisenau that the campaign of Waterloo did not end
disastrously for the Allies.

While these matters were going forward, mishaps had already begun at Wavre.   Bülow's leading division was hardly clear of the village when an accidental fire broke out in the principal street, preventing all passage through it; and the rest of the corps had to wait until the fire was burned out.   Its march was thus delayed for two whole hours.  · Pirch I. was, therefore, unable to move until past noon, and at two o'clock half of his corps was still on the east bank of the Dyle.   It had been decided by the Staff that, unless the French at Gembloux appeared before Wavre in too great force, Ziethen's corps and possibly Thielmann's also should follow Pirch I. ; but Blücher left these details to Gneisenau, being impatient for the coming battle.   He would be tied on his horse rather than miss it, he said ;  and ·at eleven o'clock the gallant old man rode off, bruised and shaken though he was, to· join Bülow.   But for his impetuous energy, Wellington might have fought the battle of Waterloo, for victory or defeat, without the help of a single Prussian soldier.

Meanwhile Grouchy for his part had received reports during the night which satisfied him that the bulk of the Prussians were moving north-west ;  and at six o'clock in the morning he sent a message to that effect to Napoleon.   " The enemy," he wrote, " is retiring on Brussels to concentrate there or to fight a battle after uniting with Wellington.   Blücher's Ist and IInd Corps seem to have gone, the one to Corbais, and other to Chaumont.   I am starting for Walhain, whence I shall go to Corbais and Wavre."   There seemed to him to be no particular reason for haste, so he did not order the foremost of his infantry to march until six o'clock ;  and, owing to the delay in the distribution of victuals, they did not start until after seven. The whole then advanced in one column upon a single road, excepting one division which, together with three brigades of cavalry, made a bend eastward in pursuance of Grouchy's ideas of the previous night.   At Walhain St. Paul Grouchy learned from a retired French

officer, or from some person passing for such, that the
Prussians who had marched through Wavre were on
the way to the plain of La Chyse, seven miles east of
the village, and were about to mass themselves there
with the object either of fighting the pursuing French
or of joining Wellington. He reckoned therefore
that he could not do better than continue his march
to Wavre, where he would be interposed between
Wellington and the Prussian army, and from whence,
if the Prussians should move towards Brussels, he
could reach the capital before they did. He wrote a
letter to this effect to Napoleon, adding that Wellington
was no doubt retreating before the Emperor ; and a
heavy distant cannonade which he heard in the direction
of Mont St. Jean an hour or two later availed not, in
spite of the remonstrances of his generals, to make
him change the direction of his march. He reasoned
once again from Napoleon's hypothesis that the
Prussians could not have recovered from their defeat,
that they had no alternative but to retire, and that, as
a natural consequence, Wellington must retreat also.

Napoleon, as the originator of this delusion, of
course cherished it with unshaken attachment. It is
said that he went round his outposts at one o'clock in
the morning to be sure that Wellington was not
escaping by stealth. Soon after dawn came in
Grouchy's letter, written at two o'clock of the 17th, to
the effect that, if the main body of the Prussians proved
to be marching on Wavre, he would follow them to
head them off from Brussels and separate them from
Wellington. All, therefore, seemed to be satisfactory.
Orders for the disposition of the troops had already
been issued on the previous day, from which it appears
that Napoleon intended to move early ; but the soil was
so much sodden after fifteen hours of nearly continuous
rain as to make the movement of artillery extremely
difficult ; and the attack was therefore deferred till nine
o'clock. At eight o'clock the Emperor breakfasted
and spoke with confidence of the issue of the coming

combat. Soult was not so sanguine, and repeated an
opinion which he had uttered on the previous morning,
that Grouchy's detachment was too strong and that
part of it should be summoned to the main army.
" You think Wellington a great general because he
beat you," answered the Emperor ; " I tell you that
he is a bad general and that the English troops are
bad troops, and that we will make short work of them."
Reille entering shortly afterwards, Napoleon asked
his opinion of the British army. " When well posted,
as Wellington knows how to post them," he answered,
" I consider it invincible by a frontal attack ; but it
is less flexible than ours. If one cannot beat them by
a direct attack, one can do so by manœuvring." The
Emperor took no notice.

Jerome presently came in and reported, on the
information of a waiter at the inn at Genappe, that one
of Wellington's staff, when dining there on the 16th,
had spoken of a projected junction between the British
and the Prussians at the entrance to the forest of Soignes.
" After such a battle as Ligny," answered the Emperor,
"the junction of the English and Prussians is impossible
for another two days ; besides, the Prussians have
Grouchy at their heels. It is very lucky that the
English are standing fast. I shall hammer them with
my artillery, charge them with my cavalry to make
them show themselves, and, when I am quite sure
where the actual English are, I shall go straight at
them with my Old Guard." [1] In such a frame of
mind it is small wonder that he was perfectly satisfied
with Grouchy's report of the previous night. The
Emperor informed him in reply that he was about to
attack the English at Waterloo, but gave him no
further order than to push on to Wavre and drive the
Prussians before him. Grouchy's letter of the morning,
which reached him shortly after ten o'clock, evoked
from him no further instructions. The Prussians
would need two days longer to recover themselves.

[1] *Vie Militaire du Général Foy*, pp. 278-279.

1815.
June 18.

The English were bad troops under a bad general. There was nothing more to be said.

Wellington on his side waited, apparently, until past one o'clock in the morning of the 18th before he received Blücher's letter, assuring him that at least one Prussian corps would march to his assistance in the course of the day. It is possible, indeed, that he may have received some earlier intimation which was sufficient to satisfy him ; but it is very evident that he did not at that hour count upon a decisive battle. Four letters from him, dated at three o'clock in the morning, are preserved, in each of which he alludes to the possibility that his position might be turned by way of Hal, and that Brussels might thereby be uncovered ; and, to meet such a contingency, he ordered Antwerp to be placed in a state of siege, recommending all refugees from Brussels to remove themselves thither. In the circumstances, it has astonished many that he should have taken no measures against the possibility of a retreat, to which he might be compelled either by Blücher's inability to support him or by the turning movement above mentioned. As a matter of fact, a subaltern of Vivian's brigade did receive orders on the night of the 17th to look for a road through the forest of Soignes, parallel to the main road and east of it, whereby the brigade might retire, covering the left of the army ; so it is reasonable to infer that other officers received the like instruction.[1] But the absence of any general directions in the event of a retreat shows that Wellington contemplated no immediate necessity for them. In other words, he was satisfied, either by his own judgment or by direct intimation, that he could count upon Blücher's assistance, and was resolved to stand his ground until he should be manœuvred out of it.

That he should have expected such a manœuvre round his right flank has caused general astonishment. The explanation, however, is not difficult. He fell

[1] *Waterloo Letters*, p. 196.

into Napoleon's error of overestimating the power of his own prestige. " I think," he said a few weeks later at Paris, " that if I had been Bonaparte I should have respected the English infantry more after what I must have heard of them in Spain ; and that I should not have taken the bull by the horns. I should have turned a flank, the right flank. I should have kept the English army occupied by a demonstration to attack or by slight attacks, while in fact I was moving the main army by Hal on Brussels." [1] It is objected to such a conception that it was contrary to Napoleon's whole plan of campaign, which was to separate Wellington's army from Blücher's. But this is wisdom after the event, if not indeed a begging of the whole question. We have seen from the Emperor's orders to Ney on the 16th of June that he attached great importance to the capture of Brussels, not only for its moral effect but because it would sever the British from Ostend ; and this idea is wholly incompatible with the separation of the armies of the Allies. If Napoleon had listened to the warnings of Soult and Reille — and the ablest [2] French historian of the campaign admits that he would have done well to consider them seriously—the vexed question would have been settled by the choice of the flank, western or eastern, by which he decided to turn Wellington's position. The only certain thing is that he could not have separated the British at once from their base and from the Prussians by one and the same manœuvre. The truth probably is that his projects were at no time so clear and well defined as he afterwards attempted to prove them to be.

Be that as it may, the Duke, holding firmly to his opinion, left Colville's division, less one brigade, and Prince Frederick's Netherlandish corps, together some fifteen to eighteen thousand men, at Hal and Tubize,

1815.

June 18.

---

[1] *Journal of Colonel James Stanhope.* MS. The writer says that the statement was made at a dinner at Grassini's in Paris in answer to the question of a French gentleman, and that he heard the words himself from the Duke's own mouth.     [2] Houssaye, p. 320.

nine to eleven miles west of Mont St. Jean, with orders, issued late on the 17th, to defend the position at Hal for as long as possible. In the course of the night Colville sent a staff-officer, Colonel Woodford, to Wellington for orders. Woodford arrived early in the morning of the 18th, but at a time when it was certain that a pitched battle was imminent. The Duke told him that it was too late for the division at Hal to move up, but added, " Now that you are here, stay with me." Evidently Wellington felt confident of Blücher's early appearance on the field ; nor was he unreasonable, for the Prussian advanced parties were actually visible at ten o'clock filing across the Lasnes less than four miles to the west.

The morning of the 18th broke dull and overcast. The thunder-clouds had not yet quite rained themselves out ; and, though they were rising and the weather generally tended to improve, there were scattered showers at different points of the line throughout the day.[1] The British, roused from their cheerless bivouac, busied themselves with looking to their arms and getting rid of the useless charges loaded on the previous day, too often by firing them off. The position of Mont St. Jean, or, as we may now call it, of Waterloo, had been studied by the Royal Engineers, who had drawn up plans of it before the opening of the campaign. It consists of two nearly parallel ridges, that of Mont St. Jean on the north and that of La Belle Alliance in the south, which run east and west, and enclose between them a narrow plain. This plain is more truly a minute watershed, from which two tiny rills flow east and west, making well-defined valleys for themselves when, on reaching the hamlets of Smohain on one side and Braine l'Alleud on the other, they change their course to a northerly direction.

---

[1] The contradictory reports of the weather during the day from various quarters are most easily explained in this way. Every one knows by experience how long it is before the last drop falls after a heavy thunderstorm.

There rises from it, however, a secondary ridge, which
runs from a point about seven hundred yards north of
La Belle Alliance for about half a mile north-westward.
The difference in elevation between the highest and
the lowest points of the plain does not exceed sixty feet,
and the gradients are nowhere so severe as to check
the speed of a galloping horse either up or down.
The ground was open and unfenced, and in the summer
of 1815 was for the most part covered with tall waving
rye.   Straight through the centre of the position runs
the road from Brussels to Charleroi, marked on the
southern ridge by the farm of La Belle Alliance and
on the northern by that of La Haye Sainte, which
stand about eleven hundred yards apart.   About three
hundred yards north of La Haye Sainte this road
crosses another, running east and west from Ohain to
Braine l'Alleud, and then turns slightly westward past
the farm and hamlet of Mont St. Jean to the village
of Waterloo, where it enters the forest of Soignes and
runs through it to Brussels.

The heights of Mont St. Jean, which had been
chosen by Wellington for his battle-ground, offered
advantages which were well suited to his defensive
tactics.   The forward or southern slope was a fairly
steep glacis, and the reverse slope was easy, so that all
movements in rear of the fighting line were concealed.
Along the summit, in places slightly in rear of it, ran
the cross-road, already mentioned, from Braine l'Alleud
to Ohain, screened, eastward of La Haye Sainte, on
each side by thick hedges which were impenetrable
by cavalry, and passing through a succession of cuttings
six or seven feet deep on the way westward to Braine
l'Alleud.   In advance of the right centre stands the
mansion of Hougoumont, which, with its grounds,
covered a rectangular space some five hundred yards
square, enclosed with hedges.   From north to south
more than half of this area was covered by a park, the
western part of which was coppice and the eastern
open ground.   Near the north-western angle stands

the house with its chapel, its extensive outbuildings, and its large garden, walled on the south and east sides; the whole being surrounded on the north, and more extensively on the east, by a fenced orchard. In the centre of the position La Haye Sainte, a quadrangle stoutly built of stone, was shielded on the north by a terraced kitchen-garden, and on the south by a long belt of enclosed orchard which ran along the western side of the Brussels road, and flanked it for over two hundred and fifty yards. To the rear of the farm and on the eastern side of the road were a gravel-pit and a mound, shut in at the back by a hedge which adjoined the road. The road itself was blocked by one abatis at the end of the pit, and by another in line with the south wall of the farm. On the left of the position the farms of Papelotte and La Haie, together with the hamlet of Smohain and the mansion of Frischermont, presented a third fortified post which, like Hougoumont and La Haye Sainte, thrust themselves out like bastions in advance of the main array. The general form of the position was concave, presenting to any assailant the difficult problem of attacking a shallow re-entrant angle.

The extreme left of the line was occupied by Vivian's brigade of light cavalry, with Vandeleur's brigade immediately on its right. Then, in succession from left to right, came the Hanoverian infantry brigades of Vincke and Best, Pack's British, Bijlandt's Netherlanders, and Kempt's British, the right-hand battalion of this last leaning its right flank upon the Brussels road. Immediately on the west side of this road stood Ompteda's brigade of the German Legion, and next to them Kielmansegge's Hanoverians and Colin Halkett's British, the whole composing Charles Alten's division. On the right of Halkett, upon the hill in rear of Hougoumont, stood in succession Maitland's and Byng's brigades of Guards.[1] On the right of

[1] Stanhope of 3/1st Guards says in his journal, "When the battle began we had two or three squares between us and the 3rd Division;

Byng, astride the road from Nivelle to Brussels, was
Mitchell's brigade, lining the road which runs westward
from that road to Braine l'Alleud.  On the plateau
behind Mitchell was massed Clinton's division, and,
in rear of Clinton again, the Brunswick contingent was
held in reserve at the village of Merbe Braine.  Lastly
Chassé's Netherlandish Division, with sixteen guns,
held Braine l'Alleud, having one brigade thrown
forward in advance of the village and at right angles
to the main line of battle.  Wellington to the very
end was nervous for his right flank.

The only infantry in second line near the centre
were Kruse's three Nassau battalions in rear of Alten's
division, and Lambert's British brigade, just returned
from America, which did not reach the field until
eleven o'clock and was then stationed at the cross-roads
just in front of Mont St. Jean.  The cavalry was for
the most part massed in rear of the centre, the Household and Union brigades under Somerset and Ponsonby
being immediately to west and east of the Brussels
road, with Van Merlen's Netherlanders to the rear of
Somerset, Dörnberg's and Arentschild's brigades to
Somerset's right, and Trip's and de Ghigny's Netherlanders immediately behind the Household and Union
brigades.  Grant's brigade stood behind the Guards,
with one squadron of the Fifteenth Hussars covering
Mitchell's right flank.

Of the artillery six mounted batteries were with the
cavalry brigades ; the two Brunswick batteries were
with their own contingent, and Bean's, Sinclair's and
Braun's batteries were in reserve about Mont St. Jean.
Ross's battery was on the high ground behind La Haye
Sainte, with two guns pointing down the road; Rogers's
and Cleeves's were in front of Alten's division;
Kuhlmann's and Sandham's in front of the Guards;

---

before it ended, the red-coats were the nearest battalion." The detail
is not very important though it is curious : and the memory of blue
coats interposed between two masses of red is likely to be correct.

Sympher's and Bolton's in reserve with Clinton's division.

Of the advanced posts, Hougoumont was held by four light companies of the Guards, two hundred Hanoverians from Kielmansegge's brigade and one of Prince Bernhard's Nassau battalions. La Haye Sainte was entrusted to the 2nd Light Battalion of the German Legion under Major Baring ; two companies of the Ninety-fifth Rifles occupying the gravel-pit. Smohain, Papelotte, La Haie and Frischermont were occupied by the four remaining battalions of Prince Bernhard's brigade.

The total number of Wellington's army amounted to about sixty-three thousand men,[1] of which twenty-one thousand were British, five thousand of the German Legion, nearly eleven thousand Hanoverians, fifty-five hundred Brunswickers, three thousand Nassauers and nearly seventeen thousand Netherlanders. The cannon numbered one hundred and fifty-six, seventy-eight of them British, eighteen of the German Legion and thirty-two Netherlandish. Thanks to the importunity of Sir Augustus Frazer, three out of the seven mounted batteries were furnished with nine-pounder in lieu of six-pounder guns. Whinyates's battery was provided with eight hundred rockets in addition to its field-pieces ; but, in spite of Wellington's repeated representations from the Peninsula, there were no cannon on the side of the Allies that could match Napoleon's favourite twelve-pounders.

It will be observed that in this line of battle the corps, into which the army had been originally organised, were broken up, or any rate disregarded, probably with the object of depriving the Prince of Orange of the definite command of any large number of troops. The Prince had given sufficient trouble at Quatre-Bras with his mischievous interference ; and the British troops would have lost much of their confidence if they had thought that they were still to be

[1] Houssaye gives him 67,700 men and 174 guns.

subjected to the caprice of so unskilful a commander.
It will be remarked likewise that Wellington was
careful to intersperse the foreign troops among the
British, leaving them nowhere without red-coats close
at hand ; while the Netherlanders, with the exception
of Bijlandt's brigade, which lay between Pack's and
Kempt's, were carefully ensconced in the villages on
the extreme flanks. " Form as usual " had been the
Duke's sole direction to his divisional generals ; and
accordingly they had drawn up their troops in rear of
the crest of the ridge, leaving the forward slope to be
disputed only by their massed light companies under
a field-officer. Bijlandt's brigade, however, not understanding the arrangement, placed itself in line with
the skirmishers. No field-works were thrown up on
any part of the line, though no doubt they would have
been of great advantage. Wellington on the night
of the 17th ordered a company of engineers to come
over from Hal and fortify Braine l'Alleud; but the
men lost their way in the dark and arrived too late.
Any attempts to entrench the ground on the morning
of the 18th were frustrated by want of tools, or in
other words by bad management. Embrasures had,
however, been cut in the hedges for the guns, and both
Hougoumont and La Haye Sainte had been more or
less prepared for defence. The main buildings and
the garden wall at Hougoumont had indeed been made
fairly strong, and at La Haye Sainte the walls had been
loopholed ; but both posts might with a little work
have been made more formidable. It appears that
the Duke forbade any preliminary fortification lest
his intentions should be thereby betrayed.

Napoleon's line of battle was as follows: On the
right stood d'Erlon's corps, with its eastern flank
covered by Jacquinot's cavalry division. Of the
infantry Durutte's stood on the extreme right, and
next to it in succession on the left the divisions of
Marcognet, Donzelot and Quiot, the last named resting
its left flank on the Brussels road. The artillery was

posted in the intervals of brigades. West of the
road Reille's three divisions occupied the first line ;
Bachelu's division on the right, Foy's in the centre,
and Jerome's on the left, with the artillery in the front
and Piré's cavalry thrown out westward to guard
the left flank. In second line, behind d'Erlon
was Milhaud's cavalry corps, with Domont's and
Subervie's cavalry divisions massed on its left just
to east of the Brussels road. Lobau's corps was in
rear of Bachelu, with its artillery on its left flank; and
Kellermann's cavalry was extended in rear of Reille,
l'Heritier's division on the right and Roussel d'Harbal's
on the left. In the third line, and in reserve, stood the
Imperial Guard, the infantry and artillery assembled
close to the road, with the light cavalry on the right and
the heavy cavalry on the left. The batteries of horse-
artillery were attached each to its division of cavalry.
In all Napoleon counted about seventy thousand [1] men,
including fifty-two thousand infantry and fifteen
thousand cavalry, with two hundred and sixty-six guns.
He had thus a great superiority in the matter of artillery,
which was even more marked in the weight of metal
than in the number of guns.

The massing of troops on and about the road
revealed his intention of making his principal onset,
as at Ligny, upon his enemy's centre ; which, indeed,
he announced in his last orders, issued at about eleven
o'clock. In these he said plainly that the attack would
be delivered upon Mont St. Jean at the intersection
of the roads by d'Erlon's corps, and that the twelve-
pounder batteries of the 1st, 2nd and 6th Corps,
twenty-four guns in all, would be massed together in
support of it. The assault was to be opened by Quiot's
division, on the left, whose left flank would be covered
by a simultaneous advance of Reille's corps ; and the
sappers of the 1st Corps were to be ready to barricade
the village of Mont St. Jean. Wellington, on the

---

[1] Houssaye gives the figure at 74,000. I have reduced this, as I
have Houssaye's total of Wellington's army, by 4000.

contrary, had concentrated the best of his troops, the 1815.
Guards and Clinton's division, on his right, leaving the June 18.
defence of his centre to Ompteda's brigade of the Legion,
and to Picton's division, which last had suffered very
heavily at Quatre-Bras.   Strangely enough, as events
turned out, the battle was conducted far more according
to the preconception of Wellington than of Napoleon.

The time for this attack was fixed for one o'clock
in the afternoon.   The Emperor's original instructions
had been that all troops should be in their appointed
stations by nine o'clock ; but this was found to be
impossible.   It took much time to gather in the
scattered bodies that had halted between Genappe
and Plancenoit during the miserable night of the 17th.
Reille's corps started, according to his account, from
Genappe at daybreak, but did not pass Napoleon's
head-quarters—a march of three miles—until nine.
The Guard, according to one authority, did not break
up its bivouac until ten, and Durutte reported that he
did not take his place on the field until nearly noon.[1]
It was natural that the French commanders should
give their drenched and exhausted men some time to
clean their arms and cook their breakfasts ; but it is
probable, looking to the complaints of marauding
made by several French officers, that it took much
time, in at any rate some regiments, to assemble the
soldiers together, and that it was the indiscipline of his
army, countenanced through many campaigns by the
practice of living on the country, which was the true
cause of Napoleon's delay in opening the battle of
Waterloo.   He might of course have begun the action
with such troops as he had on the field, but he judged
it wiser to wait until all were practically present, no
doubt comforting himself, quite reasonably, with the
reflection that every hour would improve the ground
for the movement of his cavalry and still more of his
artillery.

Having ridden down the line of his soldiers, who

[1] See Houssaye, pp. 316-318.

received him with wild enthusiasm, the Emperor
shortly after eleven o'clock decided to make a demonstration on the Allied flanks, perhaps with some hope
of inducing Wellington to weaken his centre.   Accordingly Jacquinot's cavalry made a show of turning the
Allied left about Frischermont, while Reille ordered
Jerome's division to advance upon the approaches to
Hougoumont.   Jacquinot was speedily turned back,
with some slight loss, by the muskets and cannon of
the Nassauers ;  but Jerome's column advanced steadily
towards the south-western angle of the enclosure, and
threw out a cloud of skirmishers to cover the opening
of the attack.   As the French masses came into sight,
three British batteries from the left rear of Hougoumont
opened upon them with such effect that the columns
swerved off to their left.   Part of Reille's cannon then
came into action and were supported, pursuant to an
order from Napoleon, by Kellermann's mounted
batteries.   The duel of artillery became hot ;  and
Bauduin's brigade, advancing in echelon of battalions
from the left, plunged down, not without heavy loss,
into the hollow beneath the southern border of the
coppice.   Piré's cavalry covered their left flank as they
moved.   With Jerome and Bauduin at their head,
some of the French leaped into the wood and engaged the Nassauers and Hanoverians who were
holding the border.   Twice the Allied sharp-shooters
drove the enemy out into the open, and Bauduin
himself was killed at the very outset.   But the French
skirmishers, continually strengthened as their supports
came up, presently established their footing within the
coppice ; and, though both Nassauers and Hanoverians
fought stoutly as they retired from tree to tree, they
were pressed back into the orchard.   The French
then advanced rapidly through the wood and over the
park in pursuit, but were checked at the wall of the
garden, which had been pierced by two tiers of loop-
holes and was held by a company of the Coldstream
Guards.   Strive as they might with the utmost

gallantry to scale the wall, the French were shot down
at every point by a murderous fire. Bull's howitzer
battery by Wellington's orders began to throw shells
into the wood with great effect. The Guards counter-
attacked, the Hanoverians and Nassauers seem to
have rallied to their support, and the French were
driven back with heavy loss upon their supports.

1815.
June 18.

A fortified post, when strenuously defended, frequently assumes in the eyes of the assailants an
importance out of all proportion to its true tactical
value. If the centre of the Allied line were pierced,
pursuant to Napoleon's design, Hougoumont would
become untenable on the spot. There was no occasion,
therefore, for the French to do more than occupy the
wood, at once menacing the garrison of the mansion
and barring the way to an offensive movement of the
Allies. But Jerome, nettled at his repulse, called up
Soye's brigade to renew the attack in the coppice, and
directed the remains of Bauduin's to turn the buildings
by the western side. The French stormed forward
with the greatest gallantry, driving the Nassauers before
them ; but a party of the light companies of the
Coldstream and Third Guards, taking shelter behind
a lane and a haystack below the south-western corner
of the mansion, resisted desperately. At length, the
haystack being ablaze and their retreat nearly cut off,
these ran back to the gateway in the northern front of
the buildings and took refuge in the courtyard, where
they began hastily to barricade the gate with whatever
came first to hand. A French subaltern of the 1st
Light snatched an axe from one of his pioneers and,
swinging it with gigantic strength, broke down the bars.
A few men rushed after him into the courtyard, but,
after a brief though desperate struggle, four officers
and a sergeant of the Coldstream succeeded by sheer
bodily strength in closing the gate; and the little band
of French soldiers, with the intrepid subaltern [1] among

---

[1] His name was Legros. Houssaye calls him lieutenant ; but it
appears from Martineau's list that he was only a sub-lieutenant.

them, was slain to a man. Others of Jerome's skirmishers swept round the north side of the buildings, and others again, extending themselves to westward, crept up unseen through the tall rye and opening fire upon Smith's British battery, which was unlimbered above them, compelled it to retire. Four companies of the Coldstream under Colonel Woodford, however, now came up and, driving off the skirmishers first, fell next upon the flank of the 1st Light. Caught between two fires, from within the wall and without, the French gave way immediately. Some of Soye's men, attempting to debouch from the wood into the orchard, were likewise charged by the light companies of the First Guards under Lord Saltoun and hurled back in disorder. Woodford seized the moment to strengthen the garrison within the buildings ; and Hougoumont was for the present safe.

By this time Napoleon's dispositions for his main attack were nearly if not quite complete ; but still Jerome chose to think that his one corner of the field was the most important. He had by this time taken the keen edge off most of the seven battalions of Bauduin's brigade, which had suffered only trifling loss at Quatre-Bras, and off the one regiment of Soye's brigade which had not been severely punished in that action. But, persisting in his onslaught, he now called battalion after battalion of Foy's division into action, making use presumably of Gauthier's brigade, for Jamin's had lost over forty officers and from six to seven hundred men on the 16th. Jerome now sent his skirmishers to creep along the eastern hedge of the park, in order to turn the enclosures by the east, while the troops in the wood advanced again to a gap in the fence which separated the coppice from the orchard. These last met and forced back Saltoun's light companies of the First Guards, which fell back slowly from tree to tree, drawing their assailants under the fire of the red-coats that lined the eastern wall of the garden. At the same time Wellington sent two companies of the Third

Guards down the outer hedge to meet the French
flanking parties upon the eastern side ; and after a
sharp fight the enemy was again driven back, though
the British line of defence was by this time contracted
to the southern hedge of the orchard and the southern
wall of the garden.

It was now somewhat past one o'clock.   Shortly
before one, Ney, who was in charge of Napoleon's
main attack, had sent a message to say that all was ready,
when the Emperor, who had taken his station on a
high knoll in front of the farm of Rossomme, close to
the Brussels road, observed a column of troops, some
five or six miles to north-east, emerging from the wood
of Chapelle St. Lambert.   Uncertain what they might
be, he sent off a detachment of cavalry to ascertain,
when a Prussian hussar, captured by a French patrol
about Lasnes, was brought to him.   This man, who
was extremely communicative, reported that the column
just observed was Bülow's vanguard, and that the
entire Prussian army had been assembled on the
previous night at Wavre.   The Emperor, who had
already written to Grouchy, ordering him to close in
towards the main French army, now added the information gained from the Prussian prisoner, with injunctions
to hasten the movement and crush Bülow, while Soult
appended the further explanation, " Manœuvre so as
to join our right."   Napoleon then sent out Subervie's
and Domont's divisions of light cavalry to observe the
movements of the Prussians, occupy the passages by
which they would debouch, and join hands with
Grouchy's columns as soon as they should appear.
Lobau's corps was likewise detached to support this
cavalry in some position where it could check the
advance of this new enemy.   The total number of
troops thus withdrawn from the field amounted to
some eight thousand infantry and three thousand
cavalry, with thirty-two guns.

Before the last orders had been given, the French
guns opened fire to cover the great advance upon

1815.  Wellington's left centre. No fewer than eighty
June 18.  pieces, twenty-four of them the Emperor's favourite
twelve-pounders, had been massed about and before
La Belle Alliance, and were now raining round-shot
upon the opposite slope as fast as the gunners could
load them.   At about half-past one d'Erlon's infantry
began to move in echelon of divisions from the left,
at intervals of a quarter of a mile between divisions.
Quiot's led the way immediately on the east side of
the Brussels road; and then followed in succession to
the right the divisions of Donzelot, Marcognet and
Durutte, the whole numbering some sixteen thousand
men.   Quiot's division was formed with its two
brigades side by side, each brigade in close column
of battalions.   The remainder were simply massed in
close column of battalions, three ranks deep ; consequently, each division, being made up of eight battalions
of a strength varying from four hundred and fifty to
six hundred men, took the form of a dense mass with
a front of one hundred and seventy to two hundred men and a depth of twenty-four men.   The inevitable result was that out of some four thousand
muskets only four hundred at most were in the firing
line.   This was an old fault, for which the French had
suffered a score of times in the Peninsula ; but it was
aggravated in this instance by closing up the battalions
until they practically made only one body, twenty-four
ranks deep, without leaving any distance between them
for deployment.   Indeed it is difficult to see how these
divisions could have been deployed at all unless the
battalions had filed to the right or left by threes, which
was an extremely awkward, if not impossible, manœuvre
under a heavy fire.   To whose instructions this formation was due does not appear ; but Ney, who was
in command of the attack, d'Erlon, who was in command of the corps, Quiot and Marcognet, the divisional leaders, had all of them served in Spain, and
should have known better than to match men so
clumsily arrayed against British troops in position.

1815.
June 18. However, d'Erlon's corps, having been defrauded of its share of battle on the 16th, was eager for the fight, and advanced with loud shouts to the attack.

As the French columns drew near the hostile line, they threw out skirmishers ; and, as Quiot's division approached La Haye Sainte, the left brigade inclined slightly to the left to attack the farm, while the right brigade continued its advance on the east side of the road. Swarming into the orchard the French engaged three companies of the 2nd Light Battalion of the Legion, which received them with a biting fire, but were borne back by sheer weight of numbers into the barn. On the western side of the orchard, however, two companies of the 1st Light Battalion and one of Hanoverian rifles poured destructive volleys into the flank of the advancing enemy ; and, Kielmansegge having detached a light battalion to the assistance of the garrison, Baring led his men to a counter-attack. But Napoleon had detached Travers's brigade of cuirassiers to cover the left flank of Quiot, and these, coming suddenly upon the skirmishers just as Kiel-mansegge's men were joining them, caused the whole to crowd together in confusion. The cuirassiers charged ; the counter-attack in the garden, being unsupported, gave way ; the French, sweeping round the buildings, mastered the garden on the north side ; and the Germans took refuge where best they could, some in the main position and some in the buildings. Ten of their officers fell in this unfortunate affair ; but the men in the buildings stood firm, and not all the efforts of the French could avail to dislodge them. Farther to the east the two companies of Rifles in the gravel-pit were outflanked and forced back upon their reserves on the mound ; and these in turn, sticking to their position for too long, were obliged to retreat with some precipitation across the Ohain road, where the battalion re-formed a few yards in rear of the northern hedge. Thus La Haye Sainte was totally isolated, but remained safe in the hands of its valiant garrison.

Still farther to the east, Bourgeois's brigade, struck by the fire of the Rifles from the mound and of Ross's guns in the road, had swerved to the right close to Donzelot's division, while Marcognet's division had likewise gravitated to its left towards Donzelot's, so that practically the five brigades advanced as one. Opposed to them were four battalions of Bijlandt's Netherlandish brigade (which at noon had been withdrawn in rear of the road) in first line, and the remaining battalion, flanked to its right and left by the brigades of Kempt and Pack, in second line. The Netherlanders had been much shaken, as was pardonable in raw troops, by the fire of the French artillery; and, as the masses of the French infantry drew nearer, they became more and more unsteady. Finally, after a little wild firing they broke and ran away, in spite of all the efforts of their officers, and taking shelter on the reverse slope of the position, refused, at any rate most of them, to come forward again.[1]   In their flight they carried away with them for the moment the gunners of Bijleveld's Netherlandish battery, who, in contrast to its comrades of the infantry, had stood to their pieces most valiantly. Thus a large gap was torn in the Allied line, but Picton, who had marked the wavering of the Belgians, deployed Kempt's brigade, which, holding its fire until Bourgeois was within close range—at some points, it should seem, within twenty yards—poured in a volley

---

[1] Once again, in spite of all the pleading of Le Bas and Wommersom, the testimony of all British narrators is so strong as to the misbehaviour of Bijlandt's brigade that I cannot reject it. Moreover, it seems to be confirmed rather than refuted by the official report of Colonel van Zuylen, upon which those distinguished authors so greatly rely. The Colonel ascribes the feebleness of his compatriots' fire to the fact that they were formed in two ranks instead of three, which was presumably the Prince of Orange's doing. He admits that the fall of a few files produced a gap through which the French columns advanced, that the British attacked the said columns in flank, and that he himself seconded their movement with 400 men that he had rallied. If the Netherlanders had not run away, they would have been in front of the French and more than 400 strong. Nor would the 400 have needed rallying.

and then charged with the bayonet, causing the enemy
to recoil with heavy loss. In this affray Picton
received a bullet in the temple and fell from his horse
dead.

Donzelot meanwhile pressed on to the summit of
the ridge, where he halted within forty yards of the
road in order to deploy, while his skirmishers pushed
on through the hedges that lined it. Marcognet,
thinking deployment impossible, pressed forward
without attempting to change his formation ; and
his leading battalions bored their way through the
hedges as best they could, though not without disorder.
There was nothing, to all appearance, to stop this
mass, some eight thousand strong, but Pack's brigade
of the Royals, Forty-second, Forty-fourth and Ninety-
second, which, after their losses at Quatre Bras,
counted between them barely fourteen hundred
bayonets. Leaving the Forty-fourth in reserve, Pack
formed the three remaining battalions four deep and
advanced, apparently in echelon from the left—for
the Ninety-second was the first to come into action—
to within twenty yards of the enemy, when they fired
their volleys in quick succession obliquely into the
front and flank of Marcognet's column. It does not
appear that the French were thereby checked, though,
having sustained much loss from the Allied artillery
during the advance, they may have been for the
moment staggered. According to the French account,
which seems the most probable, Marcognet's leading
battalions returned the fire, and leaped forward with
the bayonet. The British did not at once turn,
apparently, and for a few moments there was a confused and deadly fight; but the odds against them
were too strong—full four, indeed if Donzelot's
division be reckoned, full eight to one. The
moment was most critical. Bourgeois's brigade,
though shaken, had not given way past recovery.
On its left Travers's cuirassiers had re-formed after
cutting the Hanoverian battalion to pieces, and

1815. were advancing up the hill.   On its right Donzelot
June 18. was deploying on the crest of the ridge, so far
undefeated, and Marcognet was threatening to sweep
everything before him with the bayonet.   On the side
of the Allies Kempt's brigade was steady and for the
moment victorious.   The gunners, by or without
orders, were leaving their guns and hurrying to the
rear ; [1] and Pack's brigade, though not past rallying,
was certainly not standing firm.[2]   It is small wonder
that Napoleon and his staff, watching the struggle
from La Belle Alliance, thought that all was going
well.

But before the French columns reached the summit,
Uxbridge had ordered the Union Brigade farther to
the left, over against the line of Donzelot's and Marcognet's attack, and had himself taken post with the
Household Brigade immediately to west of the Brussels
road.   As Travers's cuirassiers came up the slope he
directed the King's Dragoon Guards and First Life
Guards against their front, with the Second Life
Guards in echelon to their left, and held the Blues in
reserve.   Travers's left being somewhat in advance
was first checked, but the right, pushing on, came upon
the deep cutting in the Ohain road immediately to
west of the cross-ways.   Scrambling down one side and
up the other, they were met, before they could re-form
their ranks, by the remainder of the King's Dragoon
Guards and First Life Guards.   Thus caught at a
disadvantage, the cuirassiers were broken and repulsed.
Some turned straight back and galloped down the
hill, pursued by the two British regiments ; others
inclined to their right, with the Second Life Guards
at their heels, plunged into the Brussels road, and
galloped down it as far as the barricade before La

---

[1] A sergeant of Rogers's battery actually spiked one of his guns at
this time.   *Waterloo Letters*, p. 238.
[2] See *Waterloo Letters*, pp. 72, 77, 81, 82.   The only regiment
mentioned as inclined to retire is the 92nd, but I do not believe that,
if they had retired, the others would have stood.

Haye Sainte, where, being stopped, they wheeled to
their left and fled through the open space between
the Ohain road and the gravel-pit.

Simultaneously the Union Brigade swooped down upon the heads of the French infantry columns, the Royals on the right assailing Bourgeois's brigade, the Inniskillings falling upon Donzelot and the Greys upon Marcognet. They were barely one thousand sabres altogether, but their approach was hidden from the French by the hollows of the reverse slope of the ridge, and their onslaught was as furious as it was sudden. For a moment the French masses seethed madly as the unhappy men, tightly crowded together, strove to defend themselves with musket and bayonet ; and then they dissolved into a mere pack of fugitives, flying down the slope towards their own position, with the sabres of the British dragoons playing havoc among them. As it chanced, some of Travers's cuirassiers were driven headlong into the broken ranks of the French infantry, increasing their confusion ; and the Second Life Guards joining the right of the Inniskillings, the two regiments combined in the impartial chase of horse and foot.

Seldom in all military history has there been seen a more terrific smashing of formed infantry by cavalry. It is small wonder that the British troopers became drunk and maddened by their success. Their horses were good and fairly fresh, for there had been no weight crushing down their backs all night, as in the case of the French ; the ground was in their favour ; the men could not only sit in the saddle but could ride ; and from ten to fifteen thousand French were retreating or flying before them. Quiot's troops, left in isolation at La Haye Sainte, abandoned the attack. Durutte on the extreme east, after driving the Nassauers from Papelotte and nearly reaching the crest of the ridge, found his right flank assailed by the Twelfth Light Dragoons, who drove him back in great confusion upon his reserves. It seemed as if the

British cavalry would sweep all before them ; and no
sound of voice or trumpet could make the men stop.

The Household and Union Brigades galloped on
over the plain and up the acclivity of La Belle Alliance,
until the former came under the fire of Bachelu's
division, which had been slightly advanced to cover
d'Erlon's flank during his attack, and were received
with a storm of bullets which overthrew many men
and scores of horses.  Then, seeing a compact body
of cuirassiers advancing against them, they wheeled
about and retreated, the Blues, which were less out of
hand than the rest, striving to cover the retreat.
Farther to the left the Greys, with some of the
Royals and Inniskillings, dashed into the midst of two
divisional batteries, half-way up the ridge, cut down
gunners, drivers and horses, upset the guns into a
ravine, and then swinging sharply to their left assailed
Napoleon's great battery of eighty pieces.  The Emperor ordered two regiments of Delort's cuirassiers
to attack them ; but, before these could move, the 3rd
and 4th Lancers of Jacquinot's division fell upon the
left flank of the British and bade fair to annihilate
them.  In no kind of order, and with horses blown
and exhausted, the remnants of the Union Brigade
could make little resistance nor even attempt to fly.
Sir William Ponsonby was borne down and killed,
and indeed few of them would have escaped, had not
the Twelfth and Sixteenth Light Dragoons of Vandeleur's brigade come to their rescue, charged the French
lancers in turn, and given their comrades some respite.
Thus tardily and with difficulty the remnants of the
two brigades crawled back to their places behind La
Haye Sainte.  Of two thousand troopers and horses
that had charged, over one thousand horses and from
seven to eight hundred men were killed, wounded and
missing.  The Twelfth Light Dragoons also had
lost their Colonel, Frederick Ponsonby, who was
desperately wounded, and the strength of a whole
squadron either hurt or slain.

Over the greater part of the field there was now
a lull, except for a continuous duel of artillery, while
both sides regained their positions.  D'Erlon's losses
had been very heavy ; and both Bourgeois's brigade
and Marcognet's division were for the present unfit
for further action.  At least two thousand French
prisoners had been captured.  In one place their
muskets lay in rows on the field as if they had been
grounded by word of command ; and the panic was so
great that some of the fugitives ran as far as Genappe
before they could be stopped.[1]  Twenty or thirty
French guns had been disabled.  The eagles of the
105th and 45th were taken ; and the moral effect of
the charge of the Union Brigade was strong and permanent.  On the other hand, Donzelot's division,
though not unscathed, had retired in comparatively
good order, and the Allies had paid a heavy price for
their success.  The two finest brigades of the British
cavalry had almost ceased to exist ; and there was a
strong feeling that, if they had been supported, their
success might have been more far-reaching and more
permanent.  Uxbridge, in fact, had been unable to
resist the temptation of leading the first line of the
Household Brigade himself ; the Blues and the Greys,
which he had designed to act as reserves, had both
been drawn into the main attack ; and at the critical
moment there was no general director of the whole
movement and consequently no support at hand to
maintain the leading squadrons.  Uxbridge reproached
himself bitterly to the end of his days for his fault ;
but the mischief was done and could not be amended.
Moreover, one Hanoverian battalion had been annihilated.  Bijlandt's brigade, though the officers had
wrought their utmost to hearten the men, was to all
intent out of action; and hundreds of the Netherlandish soldiers were hidden away in the forest of
Soignes, where they lay at their ease with piled arms,
cooking their soup and smoking until the time should

1815.
June 18.

[1] Houssaye, p. 356.

1815. come for them to advance in safety or to disperse to
June 18. their homes, as the fortune of the day might dictate.

Round Hougoumont the struggle never ceased to
rage with extreme bitterness, as Foy and Jerome threw
more and more of their battalions into the fight.
Byng was obliged to relieve Saltoun by sending down
his battalion of the Third Guards, which cleared the
orchard by a counter-attack and, establishing itself
along the southern hedge, restored security.  Napoleon
then sent a battery of howitzers to play upon the
buildings, and, the shells setting fire to a barn, the
flames rapidly spread to the mansion, stables and cow-
houses.  The garrison, reinforced by a battalion of
Brunswickers and another of Duplat's brigade, none
the less continued their resistance.  The wounded
lying in the burning buildings were left perforce to
their fate in spite of many efforts to rescue them ; but
the survivors fought on.  The fire fortunately stopped
at the chapel ; the French infantry, disheartened by
many failures, no longer showed the same resolution
in attack ; and, ensconced in the chapel and in such
other out-buildings as had escaped destruction, the
defenders held grimly on to Hougoumont.

# CHAPTER V

IT was now about three o'clock. Wellington had brought Pack's brigade forward to take the place of Bijlandt's, summoned Lambert's brigade to the support of the Fifth Division, and closed in the whole of his left towards the centre. The Rifles also had reoccupied the mound at La Haye Sainte ; and two fresh companies had been sent into the buildings, the defence of the orchard being now abandoned. The Emperor now reinforced Reille's artillery by some of the Guards' twelve-pounders, making them up to thirty-four pieces, and ordered them, together with the grand battery, to play upon the right and left centre of the Allies. The cannonade was more intense than the oldest soldier among the Allies had ever experienced, and Wellington withdrew the first line along a great part of his left centre a hundred yards farther to the rear, so as to give them better shelter. Under cover of this shower of shot and shell Ney led Quiot's troops once more to the assault of La Haye Sainte, while one of Donzelot's brigades advanced, not in columns but in loose swarms, to cover his right flank. Once again the main attack failed before the steadfast defence of the German Legionaries under Baring ; and Donzelot's skirmishers, meeting Kempt's and Lambert's brigades half-way up the hill, were driven back before they could make any headway. In fact, the onset appears to have been half-hearted, perhaps because the French had not yet recovered from the

1815.
June 18.

161

1815.  shock of their previous repulse ; and in many narra-
June 18. tives of the battle it is not even mentioned.[1]

The general retrograde movement of the Allied
infantry upon the reopening of the cannonade had,
however, caught the eye of Ney, who, misconstruing it
as the beginning of a general retreat, conceived the
idea of establishing a footing on the plateau with
cavalry. He therefore summoned Farine's brigade
of Delort's division of cuirassiers ; and, when Delort
pleaded that he could take no orders except from
Milhaud, who commanded the corps, the Marshal,
much incensed, directed not only the brigade but
the entire corps to advance with him. Lefebvre-
Desnoëttes's light cavalry of the Guard followed
likewise, with or without orders ; and eight regiments
of cuirassiers, one of lancers and one of mounted
chasseurs, five thousand men in all, trotted down to
the low ground just to west of the Brussels road to
form for the attack. Wellington and his staff stood
amazed. He had looked, possibly, for a still more
formidable assault upon Hougoumont ; and, as most
of Byng's brigade had already been swallowed up by
the first attack, he had brought forward four Brunswick
battalions from Merbe Braine to fill the vacant place.
But a charge of cavalry upon unbroken infantry
seemed, after the experience of Quatre Bras, sheer
madness. The infantry, drawn up by battalions
chequerwise, received orders to form square, and the
gunners were bidden to fire to the very last moment,
and then to take shelter in the nearest squares,
removing first the near wheel from every gun and
trundling it before them to their refuge.[2]

Just before Ney set his cavalry in motion, Piré's
horse made a demonstration with both squadrons

[1] See Houssaye, p. 364. The authorities quoted by him establish
beyond doubt the fact that this second attack was delivered.

[2] This last detail is chronicled in the *Life of Sir William Gomm*,
p. 373 ; but is probably best known to the mid-Victorian generation
through the pages of Henry Kingsley's *Ravenshoe*.

and battery against the British right, drawing off the
Thirteenth Light Dragoons and Fifteenth Hussars of
Grant's brigade, as well as the Second Light Dragoons
of the Legion, to oppose it.   The trumpets then rang
out, and the noble array of horsemen began to move,
cuirassiers on the right, chasseurs and lancers on the
left, in a north-westerly direction obliquely across the
valley, so as to strike the Ohain road where it ran level
with the rest of the ground.   Their formation was in
echelon of columns of squadrons,[1] with the right,
presumably, leading ; and since their front, straitened
as it was between Hougoumont and La Haye Sainte,
can little have exceeded eight hundred yards, they
must have presented an ideal target for artillery.
Their advance cannot have been rapid, for the rye
rose well above their girths,[2] and the ground beneath
it, being still wet, must soon have been poached into
deep mud.   The pace too must have decreased as they
breasted the hill, which no doubt soon became slippery,
and such horses as had been loaded with their riders
all night must speedily have flagged.   The French
artillery necessarily ceased firing as they ascended the
ridge ;  and the French cavalry's line being oblique
to that of the Allies, Wellington's guns were able
to pour a tempest of shot not only into their front
but into their flanks, blasting away whole heads of
squadrons when they came within close range.   The
French horsemen naturally wavered, for they could
hardly move forward over the heaps of dead horses.
Indeed, opposite Mercer's battery, not far from the
north-eastern corner of the orchard of Hougoumont,
the front ranks turned and, finding themselves pressed
forward by the rear ranks, actually fought them with
blows and curses in their eagerness to ride back ;

[1] Houssaye, p. 371.

[2] I never realised how immensely heavy were the rye-crops on the
field of Waterloo until I found in the Royal Collection at Windsor
Castle nine water-colour drawings of the field, made by Denis Dighton
on the days immediately following the battle—in fact, before the dead
had been buried.

while Mercer's nine-pounders, doubly loaded with case and round-shot, riddled the seething masses from end to end.

Elsewhere the French cavalry rode into the batteries, but found themselves none the better for it. They could not carry off the guns, and they possessed no means of spiking them. They could only pass through the intervals with ranks thinned and disordered, spur their horses into some semblance of a gallop and fall upon the squares. But, the farther they went, the more their front was contracted between the cuttings of the Nivelles road and the Brussels road, so that the squadrons became crowded together and their pace was checked. Moreover, the squares being arranged chequerwise, it was impossible to assail any one of them except under a flanking fire from others. Here, therefore, as at Quatre Bras, the French cavalry was reduced to an aimless wandering in and out of the squares, suffering very heavy loss and inflicting very little damage. Uxbridge meanwhile collected six regiments from the Brunswick cavalry, Grant's, Dörnberg's and Arentschild's brigades, with which, backed by three brigades of Netherlandish cavalry, he made a counter-attack, which swept the cuirassiers clean off the plateau into the dead ground under the southern slope of the ridge.

The Allied gunners instantly ran back to their guns and replaced the wheels ; and meanwhile Wellington, ceasing to be anxious for his right, had considerably altered his dispositions in that quarter. Clinton's division was moved up from its place in reserve into the front line. Hew Halkett's Hanoverian brigade was placed as a support to the Brunswickers on Maitland's right ; the Twenty-third from Mitchell's brigade was posted in the middle of the Brunswickers to give them the countenance of a veteran regiment ; Adam's brigade was stationed on their right ; and Duplat's brigade took up its position on the slope in rear of Hougoumont to be ready to reinforce that post.

These changes appear to have been completed when the French cavalry, having rallied with amazing quickness, appeared once again upon the comb of the ridge and renewed their attack.  For the second time they trotted through an appalling fire of artillery into the deserted batteries and passed on to repeat their futile gyrations round and round the squares.  Unable to pierce the hedges of bayonets, small parties of brave men engaged the red-coated infantry with their pistols, hoping to provoke the face of some square to waste a volley upon them and so to give a reserve, which was kept in rear of them, the chance of charging an array of empty muskets.  Their efforts were fruitless.  Not a red-coat fired except by word of command.  The horses, by this time unable to trot, walked round and round the bayonets in helpless swarms till they were shot down ; and the second attack failed as completely as the first.  The French cavalry, therefore, fell back down the hill ; and as they went, two columns of Quiot's and Donzelot's infantry, which had advanced against La Haye Sainte, fell back likewise ; while some battalions of Foy's division, which had crept up into the orchard of Hougoumont to turn the flank of the garrison, were driven back into the coppice by the Third Guards.

From the heights of La Belle Alliance the appearance of the opposite plateau, with the French horsemen swarming through the batteries and about the squares, apparently masters of the ground, made many of the French think that the victory was won.  Napoleon himself may have thought so for a moment, but he was soon undeceived ; and Soult, who knew the ways of Wellington, was probably not deluded for an instant.  The Emperor realised that Ney's attack had been premature, but, being committed to it, he decided to support it, and sent orders to Kellermann and Guyot to lead their ten regiments to the charge.  Kellermann was inclined to demur ; but l'Héritier marched off his division at the trot without awaiting further orders,

1815.
June 18.

and Kellermann had no option but to follow with the other.   Napoleon, in his own narrative, declared that he wished to hold Guyot's brigade of the Guard in reserve, and tried to recall it ; but it seems certain that he did nothing of the kind.   Beyond doubt he hoped to gallop over the right centre of the Allies and finish off the battle without further ado ; and he hoped so, because he was beginning to realise that, unless he could do so, he might sustain a disastrous defeat.

Blücher had overtaken Bülow's corps at Chapelle St. Lambert at about one o'clock and had at once sent out patrols to explore the passages of the Lasnes and of Paris Wood, which covered the ground for some fifteen hundred yards, north and south, beyond it. At about two o'clock, when Bülow's rear-guard was yet an hour's march away, the patrols returned with the report that the French were still at a safe distance ; and the Field-marshal at once gave the order to march upon Plancenoit.   The roads were infamous, the descent to the Lasnes being very steep and the ascent from the stream westward even steeper ; and the men were weary after an exceedingly trying march, and weak from long fasting.   It seemed hopeless to attempt to drag guns axle-deep in mud up so heavy an incline ; but Blücher would hear of no difficulties.   Along the line of march he was cheering and encouraging his men.   " I have promised Wellington," he kept saying to them.   " You would not have me break my word." His strong will and fiery energy stimulated even the most sluggish to extreme effort ; and at about four o'clock the heads of his columns reached the western border of Paris Wood, where the two leading divisions halted in concealment.   Blücher would gladly have waited for the rest of Bülow's corps to come up; but Wellington's messages, bidding him hasten, became more and more urgent; and at half-past four the two divisions, covered by two regiments of cavalry and three light batteries, emerged from the wood right and left of the Plancenoit road.   His guns unlimbered

and opened fire upon Domont's squadrons, which, after 1815.
a dash upon the Prussian hussars, fell back slowly, June 18.
and then wheeling off right and left revealed Lobau's
corps extended in two lines astride the road, about a
mile and a half east of the highway to Brussels.  Lobau,
promptly taking the offensive, drove the Prussians
back ; and Blücher was fain to halt until the rear of
Bülow's column should close up.

Blücher's guns must have been heard both by
Wellington and Napoleon soon after half-past four.
His first engagement with Lobau must have occurred
between five and half-past five, just as Kellermann's
and Guyot's squadrons were forming in the low ground,
with the wreck of Milhaud's corps streaming back all
round them.  Milhaud's men quickly rallied behind the
new array ; and the whole moved forward once again,
sixty squadrons some nine thousand strong, all cramped
within a front which could barely have held nine
hundred horsemen, knee to knee, without any intervals
whatever.  The French batteries, as before, preluded
the attack by a terrific cannonade, which was continued
to the last moment and ceased only as Kellermann's
squadrons breasted the ascent.  Advancing on the
track of their predecessors, they could not move fast
over ground poached deep by the trampling of
thousands of hoofs, and fared no better than they.
The front ranks were torn to tatters by the Allied
artillery as they ascended the slope to the batteries, and,
when the survivors had passed by the abandoned
guns, they were sucked by a dozen channels into
the intervals between the squares, where they eddied
round and round them in streams and backwaters,
now firing their pistols, now charging resolutely in
small bodies, but always beaten off by the steady fire
from behind the bayonets.  There were squares that
sustained many attacks, but it does not appear that
one of them was broken.[1]  There was no particular

---

[1] The French (see Houssaye, p. 383) claim to have broken two or
three squares and to have taken two colours, one from a British

1815.
June 18.

reason why they should have been, for there was no thunder of hoofs growing momentarily louder, no wall of dust rushing steadily nearer, no awful emergence of maddened horses and gleaming blades in endless lines and waves from the dust-cloud, no element, in fact, of the terror which cavalry can strike into infantry even in the manœuvres of peace. Instead of all this there were simply swarms of exasperated men on weary horses, who walked round and round, fetlock-deep in mire, swearing loudly and making desperate thrusts from time to time through the hedge of bayonets, but doing very little harm and offering generally a capital target. The incessant procession of these walking cavaliers might have terrified young soldiers for a moment, but old soldiers never. Whether to young or to old it was an ordeal incomparably less trying than to lie down, either in line four deep or in square, amid the bursting shells and wicked ricochetting round-shot which earlier in the day had poured in an un-broken stream from the French batteries. Under such a fire men could only endure and hope, for there was no means of reply ; but, within squares safely closed up, the disjointed attacks of walking cuirassiers

---

battalion and one from a battalion of the German Legion. British and Legion, as is well known, have never admitted that a square was broken, much less that a colour was lost, at Waterloo. Vague claims to the capture of colours are too common in the reports of French officers during the Peninsular War to carry the slightest weight with me. The receipt of a captured British colour signed by Grouchy's aide-de-camp (quoted by Houssaye, p. 383) is something more definite, but would deserve greater credit if it stated the regiment to which the colour belonged. I have never heard of a colour lost at Waterloo ; and, as the loss of its colour by the 69th at Quatre Bras was not concealed, I do not see how such a mishap could have been kept secret by any regiment. The 9th Cuirassiers, who claim to have taken a colour at Waterloo, were engaged at Quatre Bras and may have been the captors of the 69th's colour, which may have been handed over to Grouchy as having been taken at Waterloo. The 9th lost two officers at Quatre Bras and thirteen at Waterloo : and in the general disorganisation after the latter action the mistake could easily have been made.

were not very dangerous, and afforded endless opportunities for telling return blows.

Gradually the French horsemen began to retire down the slope, first in small parties, then in broken squadrons, and finally in complete masses. The British gunners rushed back to their cannon, but had barely time to fire a few rounds into the backs of their enemies before a fresh array came up the hill with its left close to the eastern fence of Hougoumont. This was Blancard's brigade of carbineers which Kellermann, with excellent judgment, had hidden in a fold of the ground during his advance, to act as a reserve. These now advanced up the height, backed, apparently, by a brigade of cuirassiers; but at this moment Grant, having undeceived himself as to the true intent of Piré's demonstration on Wellington's extreme right, had left one squadron of the Fifteenth to watch the French horse in that quarter, and returned to his original place in rear of Hougoumont. Forming the Thirteenth Light Dragoons in line he launched them at the flank of the carbineers, and a few minutes later directed the Fifteenth Hussars upon the flank of the cuirassiers. Both charges were successful, driving the enemy down the hill upon their main body. This last, however, having rallied, now with the greatest gallantry renewed its attack; and the Thirteenth and Fifteenth were compelled to fall back, which they did with great steadiness, to the rear of the infantry.

Once again the tide of the French cavalry surged into the intervals between the squares, flooding the space up to the bayonets but there stopping and rippling round them through channels now cumbered with the corpses of man and beast, powerless to break over the immovable boulders of red-coats. No men could have showed more persistent bravery than the French troopers; but they were opposed to adversaries as stubborn as themselves. After a time, as the more daring spirits were struck down, the attack became feebler and feebler. Riders and horses were in fact exhausted. The atmosphere was still heavy and thunderous, and the crowding of a vast mass of men and horses, all alike heated by extreme exertion, made the temperature almost insupportable. A stream of dismounted cavaliers was constantly pouring to the rear ; small parties began to follow them ; the whole wavered irresolutely, then, upon the advance of the Allied cavalry, gave way and were swept over the plateau. Their losses had been frightful. Ney, having had three horses killed under him, was afoot, raging with fury. In Kellermann's corps both divisional generals and three brigadiers were wounded and the fourth brigadier was killed. In Milhaud's corps both divisional generals and three out of four brigadiers were wounded, and in the cavalry of the Guard General Guyot was wounded. Hardly a general officer was left standing, and there was not a regiment of cuirassiers which had lost less than a dozen officers. Nevertheless it seems that Ney gathered the wreck of them together for a fourth charge, which was as gallantly delivered as the condition of the horses would permit, but failed as completely as all the rest. The flower of the French cavalry had been wrecked upon a score of attenuated squares.

Ney now resorted to the tactics which he should have employed at first ; namely, to use infantry and cavalry in conjunction with each other. Wellington, anticipating some such design, had some time before ordered Chassé's Netherlandish Division to march to a hollow in rear of the Guards so as to liberate Duplat's and Adam's brigades for work in the front line, and had reinforced his artillery by two batteries. In due time two columns of Bachelu's and Foy's divisions, supported by cavalry, advanced against the centre of the Allied right wing under a heavy fire from the British guns. "It was a hail of death," wrote Foy afterwards ; and the French infantry quailed under it. Bachelu's men turned first and carried away Foy's in their flight. Foy himself was wounded, but rallied his men in the ravine to the south of Hougoumont before he left the field. The attack was then renewed and was met and checked for a time by a charge of Somerset's Household Brigade. But Trip's Netherlandish cavalry, which were in support, refused to move forward ; and, when they saw the cuirassiers moving forward against them, they turned and galloped to the rear, greatly disordering the 3rd Hussars of the Legion in their flight. The 3rd, presently rallying, charged and broke the cuirassiers immediately opposed to them, but were enveloped by others upon their flanks and were fain to retreat to the rear of the squares with very heavy loss. Uxbridge then called upon another Netherlandish regiment, the Cumberland Hussars, to move forward ; but in this corps the rawness of the men was supplemented by the cowardice of their colonel ; and, in spite of all efforts to make them stand, even out of fire, these wretched creatures galloped off to Brussels, spreading panic as they went. Meanwhile, Wellington had ordered Duplat's brigade to reinforce the right centre ; and the rifle-fire of its four light companies compelled the line of French horse to withdraw. The remainder of the brigade then came up, together with Sympher's battery, and formed squares to resist the second line of French horse ; but the French skirmishers during the attacks of the cavalry had seized the opportunity to creep up under the eastern hedge of Hougoumont to the brow of the main position, from whence they poured in a most galling fire upon the squares. Duplat fell mortally wounded, and the horses of all the mounted officers were killed ; but it was impossible for the Germans to deploy, from fear of a charge from the enemy's cavalry. The charge was presently delivered, and was manfully beaten off ; whereupon the skir- mishers swarmed forward again to ply the squares with bullets while the French mounted batteries unlimbered to scourge them with grape, so as to prepare the way for another charge.

Through this most trying ordeal the bearing of

Duplat's battalions was wholly admirable; and presently they were relieved by the advance of Adam's brigade, in two lines four deep, with Wellington himself at their head. The moment was most critical, for the gunners of the Allies had been driven from their guns, and the French skirmishers in great force had opened a very heavy fire upon Adam's advancing battalions. " Drive those fellows away," ordered the Duke calmly ; and the Seventy-first together with the eight companies of the Rifles [1] obediently drove them from the crest, halted in a slight hollow near the north-east angle of the Hougoumont enclosures and formed squares, the Seventy-first on the right, the Fifty-second in squares of wings in the centre, and the Ninety-fifth on the left. They were promptly assailed by Guyot's brigade of the Imperial Guard, but they received them with volleys so telling that after several charges the French drew off, there being few but dismounted men left to retire. Two battalions of Hew Halkett's Hanoverian brigade then advanced to the southern slope of the ridge, taking post to the rear of Duplat ; and the right centre of the Allies was thus firmly re-established.

Simultaneously Ney had directed a part of Donzelot's division upon La Haye Sainte. Baring, who was short of rifle-ammunition, sent urgent messages for a supply but could obtain none, though three additional companies were sent to reinforce his garrison. The French made a desperate attempt to break in by an unclosed doorway, opening on the south side into a barn, and, failing, set the barn itself on fire. With great readiness Baring ordered his men to fill their camp-kettles at a pond in the yard, and though many lost their lives in thus fetching water, he succeeded in extinguishing the flames. While these were thus desperately engaged with one party of the enemy, another swarm of French skirmishers advanced beyond the buildings on the western side, with the intention either of breaking in on the north side or of cutting off

[1] 2nd batt.: 6 cos. ; 3rd batt.: 2 cos.

the post altogether from the main position. Thereupon the Prince of Orange ordered the 5th and 8th
battalions of the Legion to deploy and advance ; and
the brave Germans, hoping that there would now be
an end of lying down under a heavy cannonade, ran
eagerly forward driving the French before them.
The 8th, which was in advance, was on the point of
charging with the bayonet when a body of French
cuirassiers, fresh from an unsuccessful attempt upon
Kielmansegge's squares, suddenly burst upon their
right flank by surprise and rolled them up from end
to end. The unfortunate battalion was practically
annihilated, most of its officers were killed, and the
King's colour was captured. None the less the attack
on La Haye Sainte was beaten off, and Baring with his
noble garrison remained still in proud possession.

It was now not far from six o'clock, and in due
course of time two more of Bülow's divisions had
debouched from Paris Wood. Blücher resumed his
advance against Lobau, but was met with so stout a
resistance that he was fain to abandon his frontal
attack and gain ground by manœuvring to turn his
opponent's right flank. Lobau thereupon fell back
to the level of Plancenoit, throwing one brigade into
the village. Blücher then assaulted Plancenoit from
three different points, drove out the French garrison,
entrenched himself there, and bringing forward his
artillery opened a cannonade, throwing some shot as
far as the Brussels road. Twice during the course
of these operations urgent messages came in from
Thielmann at Wavre, saying that he was attacked by
superior numbers and doubted his power to hold out
against them. But Gneisenau had a great as well as
a small side, and on this day the greatness was upper-
most. " Let Thielmann defend himself as best he
may," he answered ; " it is no matter if he be crushed,
so long as we gain the victory here."

With a new enemy pressing upon his right flank and
arrived within cannon-shot of his main line of communi-

1815. cations, Napoleon realised that no time must be lost.
June 18. He gave orders to Duhesme's division of the Young
Guard to retake Plancenoit, and directed Ney to master
La Haye Sainte at any cost. Durutte he had already
instructed to make a fresh attack upon Smohain, so
as to take pressure off Lobau. Duhesme's eight
battalions did their work nobly, driving the Prussians
from Plancenoit with irresistible dash. Ney, hurrying
to the head of the 13th Light, led them against La
Haye Sainte ; and Baring called upon his men for
yet another effort. It was a hard moment for him.
The stock of ammunition was reduced to two or three
rounds a man, and for some reason rifle-cartridges,
though frequently and pressingly sought, were still
not forthcoming. Not the less did his men promise
cheerfully to stand by him to the last ; and this new
onset of the French was met with the same gallantry
as the first. Once again the barn was set on fire and
once again the flames were extinguished ; but, as rifle
after rifle fell silent for want of ammunition, the
French gained ground. Baring, slowly retiring to the
garden, made his men return singly to the main
position, where they rejoined their regiments ; while
he himself joined two companies of the 1st Light
battalions close to the cross-roads. No men could
have borne themselves more heroically than these
defenders of La Haye Sainte ; but there was no dis-
guising the fact that, though it was no fault of theirs,
the key of Wellington's centre was lost.

Realising his advantage Ney begged the Emperor
for fresh infantry to turn it to account. " Where am
I to get them ? " answered Napoleon testily. " Do
you expect me to make them ? "[1] There was nothing
for it but to assemble the shattered remains of Donzelot's and Quiot's divisions, with the remains of the
cuirassiers, to support the attack on the centre, while
the remnants of Reille's corps were set in motion for

[1] Every one assigns a different time to this celebrated speech : but
this seems to me the most likely moment.

a supreme attempt against Hougoumont. The actual victors of La Haye Sainte were able from the garden and buildings to command the knoll by the sand-pit with their fire, and to drive away the two companies of Riflemen which held it ; and then, bringing up two guns to the bank of the high road, they poured a storm of grape upon Kempt's brigade on the other side of it. The Riflemen speedily put a stop to this by picking off the gunners ; but fresh guns were brought up to a spur over against the middle of the British right centre, which played havoc with the Allied batteries. Now a fresh column of French issued from behind the farm and, extending into a close line of skirmishers, fell upon Ompteda's devoted brigade of the Legion. Alten sent orders to Ompteda to deploy, ·if practicable, and drive these tormentors off. Ompteda, knowing that cuirassiers were lying in wait in rear of the sharp-shooters, deprecated any such measure ; but at this moment the Prince of Orange rode up and, deaf to all protestations, peremptorily ordered Ompteda to deploy. Ompteda could only obey, and placing himself at the head of the 5th battalion led it forward to the charge. The French fell back to La Haye Sainte, where they took shelter among the enclosures ; and then, as Ompteda had predicted, a regiment of cuirassiers fell suddenly upon his right flank and swept his men out of existence. The Riflemen on the other side of the road, after long hesitation from fear of hitting friends as well as foes, now poured in a volley which staggered the cuirassiers ; and the 3rd Hussars of the Legion galloping forward cleared the whole front of Ompteda's brigade until compelled by the arrival of fresh bodies of French horse to retire. In this affray Ompteda, a most gallant officer, was killed, an immolation to the ignorance and self-sufficiency of the Prince of Orange. The Prince himself was presently forced by a wound to quit the field, and none too soon. In two days he had succeeded in destroying three good battalions of the British and German infantry, each one by the repetition of the same foolish mistake.

Another body of French skirmishers now turned north-west from La Haye Sainte, threatening alike Maitland's brigade, of which the Third battalion of the First Guards, formed in square, was posted in advance of the rest, and the square of Riflemen which formed the left of Adam's brigade. Both were suffering severely when Wellington ordered the Guards to deploy and charge, which they did, re-forming square instantly as the French cavalry came up. The latter shrank from the attack, but too late to escape from the bullets of the Guards ; and then, losing their heads, they galloped along the whole front of the Fifty-second, losing scores of men from the fire of that regiment. The pressure upon the Guards was thus relieved ; but immediately afterwards the principal onslaught upon Hougoumont was developed by Reille's corps. The mansion was by this time nearly burned out, but the outhouses, except on the south side, were still aflame ; and the defenders were much harassed by the heat and smoke. Nevertheless their resistance was as strenuous as ever. The flank-companies of the Guards still held the walls and buildings. The Coldstream lined the hedge that bordered the main approach to the mansion. The Third Guards occupied the orchard, and, though driven back at first to the road beyond it, recovered themselves with the help of the light companies and the 2nd German battalion of Duplat's brigade, finally, after many vicissitudes of fortune, re-establishing their position at the front hedge of the orchard.

All therefore was well with Hougoumont ; but all was not well in the centre. From the knoll above the sand-pit—their other point of vantage—the French skirmishers poured an active and deadly fire upon the troops right and left of the Brussels road. Kempt's and Lambert's brigades, though sorely tried, replied with spirit enough, though the Twenty-seventh, lying

in square in the north-eastern angle of the cross-roads,
suffered terribly. But the survivors of Ompteda's
brigade were beginning to steal to the rear, and it was
evident that they were exhausted as a fighting force.
He would be a stern judge that would blame them,
for two out of the four battalions had been cut to
pieces and the other two cruelly punished. Kielmansegge's young battalions also were much shaken.
Alten, Colin Halkett and Ompteda had fallen; and
Kielmansegge, who was striving desperately to rally
his own men, was left in charge of the division. A
dangerous gap was, in fact, opened and slowly widening
in the British centre, and the situation was critical in
the extreme. Somerset, with the wreck of his brigade
extended in rank entire, so as to make a show, was
endeavouring to instil confidence into the Hanoverians
and to keep them in their places. He had been
ordered some time before to withdraw and to take
shelter from cannon-fire, but had answered that the
slightest movement would make the Netherlandish
cavalry, which were in support of him, turn and run.
The situation was happily saved by Vivian, who,
without orders, brought up his brigade of light
dragoons and, forming them in rear of the wavering
battalions, brought them to a stand ; and Wellington
presently brought up five Brunswick battalions from
the second line to fill the gap more thoroughly.
These last were not at first very steady ; in fact they
gave way in a body. They were not without excuse,
for they were very young soldiers and they had been led
straight into the post of greatest danger ; but through
the efforts of Wellington and other officers they were
rallied. Vandeleur's brigade was presently sent up
by Uxbridge to join Vivian ; and a very dangerous
crisis was successfully passed.

It was now seven o'clock ; and meanwhile Blücher
had not been idle. Rallying the repulsed battalions
of Bülow's corps, he made a strong counter-attack upon
Plancenoit, drove the Young Guard from it, and,

1815.
June 18.

again bringing forward his artillery, began to throw shot dangerously near to La Belle Alliance itself. Napoleon thereupon formed eleven battalions of the Guard in squares along the road from Rossomme to La Belle Alliance, and sent down two battalions of the Old Guard to retake Plancenoit. The veterans marched down in columns, plunged into the village without firing a shot, and in twenty minutes had swept every Prussian out of it, leaving it to be reoccupied by the Young Guard. Having thus, as he thought, cleared his right flank, Napoleon decided that the time was come for the final blow. He could see on his extreme right Durutte, already master of Papelotte and La Haie, preparing to ascend the slope, his own troops fighting strongly and with advantage in the centre, Hougoumont blazing on the left. All seemed to be well ; and after nearly eight hours of desperate fighting the supreme moment was at hand. He ordered Drouot to set nine battalions of the Guard in motion, keeping two at Plancenoit, and three in reserve ; and he himself rode down to lead the foremost of them into the valley. Reille and d'Erlon were instructed to advance simultaneously, with such troops as they could raise, upon the centre and upon Hougoumont.

But there was one thing which Napoleon did not and could not see. Soon after six o'clock Ziethen, after endless delays both in starting and in marching, had arrived at Ohain with his advanced guard— perhaps five thousand men—and had been met by Colonel Freemantle of Wellington's staff with a pressing request for an immediate reinforcement, even if of no more than three thousand men. Ziethen hesitated to comply until his whole corps should have come up ; and one of his staff-officers, galloping forward to judge of the reasonableness of Wellington's demand, found so many men, wounded and unwounded, making off, that he reported the British to be in retreat.

¹ *Waterloo Letters*, p. 330.

Shortly afterwards an order arrived from Blücher for
the 1st Corps to join Bülow ; and Ziethen naturally
moved his troops in that direction. Müffling, however, perceiving him from a distance, galloped at the
top of his speed to entreat him to join Wellington,
and after much hesitation contrived to persuade him.
But meanwhile much time had been lost ; and the
only advantage so far gained from Ziethen's arrival
within two miles of Wellington's left was that Vivian
had felt himself justified in quitting his post in
rear of Smohain to reinforce the centre. It was
not until the Imperial Guard was actually in motion
towards the valley that Ziethen's leading troops at
last debouched from Smohain. At the sight of them
it seems that some of the French troops began to give
way. The Emperor rallied them in person and sent
aides-de-camp flying to all parts of his line to announce
the arrival of Grouchy.

Wellington during this interval had brought forward Chassé's Netherlandish divisions from Merbe
Braine to take the place of the Brunswickers in rear of
Maitland and Colin Halkett ; and he was apprised of
the coming attack by a royalist colonel of cuirassiers
who galloped up to Colonel Colborne of the Fifty-
second and told him that Napoleon with his Guard
would be upon them in half an hour. The Duke rode
down the line between the Brussels and Nivelles roads
ordering all battalions to be ranked four deep ; and
in this formation the infantry lay down, to avoid the
cannonade with which Napoleon preluded his final
advance, and awaited the storm. By this time six
battalions of the Guard had reached the foot of the
hollow. The Emperor left one of them [1] on a slight
eminence midway between Hougoumont and La Haye
Sainte ; and the remaining five were ordered to
advance in echelon from the right, the 1st battalion
of the 3rd Grenadiers leading, followed in succession by the 4th Grenadiers, 1st and 2nd battalions of

[1] 2/3rd Grenadiers.

1815. the 3rd Chasseurs and a single battalion of the 4th
June 18. Chasseurs.

Formed each of them in a dense column with a
frontage of seventy to eighty men and a depth of at
least nine ranks,[1] the five battalions moved off in
superb order with two guns loaded with grape in the
intervals between them, five Generals at their head,
and Ney in front of all. Proceeding parallel to the
Brussels road for some distance they found their front
covered by d'Erlon's troops, which were engaged immediately to west of La Haye Sainte, and turned
obliquely to the north-west, with the result that the
right-hand battalion fell slightly to the rear of the
rest. In this order they strode into the re-entrant
angle formed by the British right centre.

By this time the Allied batteries in this quarter had
suffered so much from loss of men and disabled guns
that their fire had grown perceptibly weaker. Cleeves's
and Kuhlmann's guns had actually retired to fetch
ammunition ; Mercer's had grouped themselves into
a strange heap, the men being too much exhausted to
run them forward after each recoil ; and nowhere
was shot any too plentiful. Happily Chassé, a very
fine soldier who had won a great reputation in the
French army, called up Van der Smissen's Netherlandish battery, which came galloping forward from
the reserve, and unlimbering on the right of Lloyd
opened a rapid fire immediately. The remainder fired
round-shot and grape with all the energy of which
their few harassed and weary gunners were capable ;
and the Imperial Guards were seen to bend under the
stroke like corn smitten by the wind. Still they never
for a moment gave way, though, as the five battalions
continued to advance over the miry ground under a

[1] Houssaye thinks that the Guard attacked in squares, and there
is much evidence in favour of his contention. But although the fate
of d'Erlon's corps may have suggested this formation, I think it more
probable that the battalions were really formed in column of double
companies, which would give them the frontage and depth above
described.

continual tempest of shot, they lost their correct intervals
and distances.   The two right-hand battalions seem
to have dropped somewhat in rear, the third and fourth
battalions, reckoning from the right, united into one,
and the left-hand battalion preserved its place slightly
in rear of the centre.   Hence, apparently, it was that
the third and fourth battalions—the 3rd Chasseurs—
were the first to come into action against Maitland's
brigade of Guards.   They could see nothing of the
British line whatever except the guns, for all the red-
coats were lying down ; and they had approached to
within twenty yards when Wellington at last said,
"Now, Maitland !  Now's your time !"   Then the
old story of the Peninsular battles was repeated.   The
Guards, four ranks deep, had a front of over two
hundred and fifty men, the two columns of the Imperial
Guard a front of perhaps one hundred and fifty.   The
red-coats poured in a volley from the two foremost
ranks which tore the front and flanks of the French to
tatters, and, with the two rearmost ranks to reload for
them, continued to rain on their enemies a murderous
shower of bullets.   The senior French commanders fell
among the first ;  their men staggered, uncertain what
to do next ;  and the junior officers, instead of waving
them forward to the charge, gave the order to deploy.
It was the old mistake of Albuera.   Such an evolution
in the face of such a fire at close range was impossible.
The flank-companies tried to come forward, but in-
voluntarily shrank back before the storm of bullets.
Hesitation became unsteadiness, and unsteadiness
turned to disorder.   Wellington and Saltoun gave
the word to charge, and the red-coats lowering their
bayonets rushed forward and hurled their enemies in
confusion before them.

Observing the progress of the Guards, Halkett
threw forward the Thirty-third and Sixty-ninth to
protect their left flank ;  and it was, apparently, while
these two battalions were thus advanced that the two
right-hand battalions of the French Guard approached

Halkett's brigade. What happened at this point it is extremely difficult to ascertain. It seems that the French gave way before the first volley of the Thirtieth and Seventy-third, much to the surprise of the British,[1] but that their guns continued to play upon the red-coats with deadly effect. In an evil moment some one gave the order for the two British battalions to face about and take shelter under a bank in rear ; and the whole brigade rushed back in panic. For a short time they were so much crowded together that they could not move ; but, by the exertions of Halkett and their officers, they speedily recovered themselves, and, backed by Chassé's Belgians, repelled a second attack, either of these same battalions of the Guard or of some of Donzelot's troops. The whole incident is somewhat obscure, but it is certain that at this point of the Allied line there was great danger for a time ; and it seems probable that the first recoil of the Guard before the British volleys was due either to its previous losses from Van der Smissen's guns, or to the sight of their comrades retiring before Maitland's Guards.

Maitland's brigade, indeed, was following up its success triumphantly ; but, before it had advanced fifty yards, the brigadier observed the 4th Chasseurs— the left-hand battalion of the French array—coming up to the rescue of their comrades upon his right flank. He gave the word to retire, but his voice was lost in the din of battle, and the order came to his men in the shape of " Form Square." The flank-companies of his battalions accordingly doubled back to take their place in square. The officers, who saw the mistake, tried to set it right ; and in the general bewilderment the whole brigade ran back, disordered by the incomplete manœuvre, to its original station, where it halted instantly at the word of command and re-formed with perfect steadiness and calm. Wellington, perceiving the mishap, ordered the Rifles of Adam's brigade to molest the flank of the 4th Chasseurs ; but

[1] *Waterloo Letters*, p. 330.

1815.
June 18.

Colborne, anticipating him, led down the Fifty-second, and formed it, four deep, along the whole length of its flank, to " make the column feel his fire." Whether the 3rd Chasseurs had rallied in rear of the 4th, or whether some of Reille's troops had come up and joined it, is uncertain ; but it should appear that there was certainly more than one battalion opposed to Colborne. As he formed his array the French opened a fire upon him which brought down one hundred and fifty men ; but his answering volley was crushing, and was followed by a charge with the bayonet, under which the French broke and gave way. The Fifty-second now continued their advance straight across the battlefield from west to east, gradually inclining to their right as the French turned instinctively towards their original position at La Belle Alliance. The Rifles and Seventy-first were hastening to form on their left and right; and Colborne, bethinking himself of his danger from a possible attack of cavalry, was disposed to halt. " No, no," shouted Wellington. " Go on ; go on."

The Duke was right. The defeat of the Guard had shaken the French in every part of the field. The long period of passive endurance was past, and the time for a general counter-attack was come. While the Imperial Guard was making its onslaught upon Wellington, part of Pirch I.'s corps had joined Blücher, who had promptly ordered a fresh assault upon Plancenoit. Ziethen in the meantime had beaten back Durutte, whose artillery had opened upon Smohain; and, as his infantry came up, drove him farther from La Haie and Papelotte. Wellington, leaving Colborne to take care of himself, ordered Vivian to move down across the scene of the conflict between the British and the Imperial Guard, so as to complete the discomfiture of the enemy, and then galloped, together with a single staff-officer, from Hougoumont to the left of his line to order a general advance. When he reached Kempt and Lambert and bade them move, Harry

1815.
June 18.
Smith, Lambert's brigade-major, was fain to ask in what direction the movement was to be, for there was for the moment a lull in the firing and the smoke was so thick that nothing could be seen. " Right ahead, to be sure," answered the Duke ; and presently the smoke cleared away, and a gleam of light flashed down from the setting sun. The Duke raised his hat high in air, and at his signal the red-coats stirred at last from the ground to which they had been rooted, and broke into a majestic advance.

Under this combined counter-attack of the British, Hanoverians, Netherlanders and Prussians, the French gave way at every point.[1]   Whole battalions, which had been brought back from La Belle Alliance after being engaged, left their arms piled and ran away. Wellington's progress exposed Durutte's flank to the onset of Ziethen; the defeat of Durutte uncovered the flank of Lobau; and by a supreme effort Blücher drove the Guard, after a most noble and glorious resistance, from Plancenoit. All was now confusion except in the three squares of the Old Guard which Napoleon had held in reserve, and in the single regiment of Horse-grenadiers. Vivian, after dispersing a mass of broken infantry, had charged and routed some cavalry that attempted to check him; and he now broke into one square of infantry and passed on, cutting down the fugitives by scores. Vandeleur followed him; and it was left chiefly to Colborne and the Artillery to deal with the squares of the Old Guard, which retreated steadily and in perfect order, frequently turning to bay. Shortly after nine Blücher and Wellington met near La Belle Alliance, and it was arranged that the Prussians should take up the pursuit. Vivian pleaded that his brigade was still fresh, but was met by the rejoinder that the British had done a hard day's work, and that he must put his men into bivouac. The energy and resource with which the Prussians pushed the pursuit has become a proverb ; but indeed the panic was such

[1] Lord Ellesmere's *Personal Recollections of Wellington*, p. 101.

1815.

June 18.

that there was little attempt at a rally.   Napoleon himself, after journeying for a short distance in his carriage,
took to his horse again and so escaped capture.   Little
effort was made to check the pursuers at the defile of
Genappe ; and, as no rear-guard had been formed, the
task of the Prussian cavalry, lighted by the moon, was
an easy one.   Insatiable in their vengeance for many
evils suffered since Jena, the Prussians pressed the
fugitives hard.   Nine several times the weary French
tried to bivouac, to be roused up to renewed flight by
the merest handful of men, indeed by the mere sound
of trumpet or drum.   The chase lay over the field of
Quatre Bras, where the hideous spectacle of the still
unburied dead struck the fugitives with fresh horror
and panic.   Not until he reached Frasnes did Gneisenau
give the order to halt.   The French army that had
fought at Waterloo had, as a military body, literally
ceased to exist.

# CHAPTER VI

THE Allied troops bivouacked on the ground that they had won, all except the Thirty-third and Sixty-ninth, weak young battalions which, having been cruelly tried both at Quatre Bras and Waterloo, had reached the limit of their endurance. Wellington himself rode back silently at a walk to Waterloo followed by the remnant of his staff, one and all " wearing rather the aspect of a funeral train than of victory in one of the most important battles ever fought." Between ten and eleven [1] he reached the inn where were his head-quarters, and on dismounting patted his chestnut thoroughbred, Copenhagen, approvingly on the quarter. The horse, who had carried his master for fourteen or fifteen hours and must have galloped more miles than are generally traversed in the longest day's hunting, lashed out with his near hind leg as if he had only just left the stable; and this was the last danger that was escaped by the Duke on the 18th of June. He sat down to write his despatch ; and later on, the first casualty-lists were brought to him. He listened as the long tale of names was read to him, and, before it was half rehearsed, broke down and cried. Fitzroy Somerset had been wounded by his side; two more of his personal staff, Canning and Gordon, had been killed; Barnes, the Adjutant-general, Elley his deputy, and De Lancey,

---

[1] Jackson (*Reminiscences of a Staff Officer*) says after ten ; the Duke himself said, a year after the event (*Supp. Desp.* x. 509), between eleven and twelve.

the Quarter-master-general, had all of them been
wounded, the last, as it proved, mortally. Among the
generals, Picton, who had been struck by a bullet at
Quatre Bras but had concealed the hurt, William
Ponsonby, Duplat and Christian Ompteda had been
killed ; Uxbridge, together with all four of his aides-
de-camp, Cooke, Kempt, Pack, Colquhoun Grant,
Adam and Colin Halkett, had been wounded. Out
of fifty assistants in the departments of the Adjutant
and the Quarter-master-general, two had been killed
and thirteen wounded. Of sixteen officers commanding regiments of cavalry, three had been killed and
seven wounded ; of twenty-five commanders of
battalions, one had been killed and eleven wounded.
In the four squadrons of the Life Guards thirteen
officers had fallen ; in the King's Dragoon Guards
eleven, in the Royals thirteen, in the Greys sixteen,
in the Seventh Hussars twelve, and in the Fifteenth
Hussars nine. In the two battalions of the First
Guards seventeen officers had been killed or wounded,
besides fourteen at Quatre Bras ; in the Coldstream
ten, and in the Scots Guards twelve ; in the Twenty-
third, ten ; in the Twenty-seventh, nine out of twenty
present; in the Thirtieth, sixteen, besides two at Quatre
Bras; in the Thirty-second, nine, besides twenty-two at
Quatre Bras; in the Thirty-third, nine, besides twelve
at Quatre Bras ; in the Fortieth, eleven ; in the Fifty-
second, ten; in the Sixty-ninth, six, besides five at Quatre
Bras ; in the Seventy-first, fourteen ; in the Seventy-
third, seventeen, besides four at Quatre Bras ; in the
Seventy-ninth, thirteen, besides seventeen at Quatre
Bras ; in the Ninety-second, six, besides twenty at
Quatre Bras ; and in the two battalions of the Ninety-
fifth,[1] thirty, besides four at Quatre Bras. Lastly, in the
Royal Artillery, out of some eighty officers present, seven
had been killed and fifteen wounded on the 16th and
18th, and among the slain was Major Norman Ramsay.

1815.

June 18.

[1] There were present the 1st battalion, six companies of the 2nd,
two companies of the 3rd.

Nor had the men suffered less severely than the officers. In the Household Cavalry Brigade the non-commissioned officers and men killed and wounded numbered over one hundred and eighty ; and some two hundred and thirty were missing, having been taken prisoners. In the Union Brigade the dead alone exceeded two hundred and fifty and the wounded were little short of three hundred. The Twelfth Light Dragoons had over one hundred and ten casualties of all ranks, and the Seventh Hussars over one hundred and fifty. In the infantry, the Second battalion of the First Guards lost nearly one hundred and fifty non-commissioned officers and men, and the Third battalion three hundred and twenty-four; so that the First Guards lost altogether at Quatre Bras and Waterloo not far from eleven hundred rank and file out of two thousand present, and not a single man of them taken prisoner. The Coldstream lost two hundred and eighty-two and the Third Guards two hundred and fifteen rank and file out of about a thousand present, and escaped cheaply. Of the brigades that had been engaged at Quatre Bras, Halkett's began the battle of Waterloo with nineteen hundred and fifty bayonets and came out with fourteen hundred and thirty ; Kempt's with nineteen hundred came out with just over thirteen hundred ; Pack's with fourteen hundred came out with nine hundred and seventy-five. Among the individual battalions the Twenty-eighth had since the 16th lost two-fifths of its numbers, the Royals and Thirty-second one-half, the Forty-second, Seventy-ninth and Ninety-second considerably more than one-half. The battalions that were engaged at Waterloo only did not suffer so severely, except the eight companies of the second and third battalions of Rifles, which lost nearly one-third, and the Twenty-seventh, which, pent up in square by the cross-roads above La Haye Sainte, was cruelly punished without an opportunity of firing a shot in reply. Out of seven hundred rank and file of the Twenty-seventh present no fewer than ninety-six were killed outright and three hundred and fifty wounded—a noble record of stubborn endurance.

The battalions of the German Legion and the Hanoverians had not escaped more lightly than the majority of the British, having most of them casualties varying from one-fourth to one-third of their strength; while the gaps in the 2nd Light Battalion of the Legion amounted very nearly to one man in two. The proportion of the fallen among the Brunswickers was on the whole slightly smaller, for, even reckoning their previous losses at Quatre Bras, there was not one in which the proportion of slain or hurt amounted to one-third of their strength. Nevertheless, among the eight battalions one showed nearly two hundred casualties, two over one hundred and seventy, and a fourth over one hundred and fifty. Of the Netherlanders it is more difficult to speak. The Prince of Orange stated their casualties at about forty-two hundred for the three days of the 15th, 16th and 18th of June; half of which, roughly speaking, were returned as " killed or missing " and the other half as wounded. From another table it appears that nearly sixteen hundred of the forty-two hundred were missing, and over twelve hundred slightly wounded. As the whole number of the British missing in the two actions little exceeded six hundred, and the majority of these were taken prisoners in the wild charge of the Household and Union Brigades of cavalry, there is evidently something here which needs explanation.

However, the main point was that Wellington's army had lost in all close upon fifteen thousand men, or not far from a fourth of its numbers, and that none the less it must continue to advance. So worn out was every soul after the battle that the chief artillery officer never thought of collecting the captured guns, which with characteristic arrogance and dishonesty the Prussians promptly appropriated to themselves.

1815. In deference to Wellington's protests, however, they
June 18. gave up half of these, which left one hundred and
twenty - two pieces in the Duke's hands.[1]  A weary
staff - officer rode out at one in the morning of the
June 19. 19th, bearing a terse order for the troops to move
to Nivelles at daylight ;[2] and a few hours later the
Duke betook himself to Brussels to see to various
matters.  A vast mass of stragglers of all nations had
found their way to the city, some in charge of wounded
men, more from unmixed solicitude for their own
safety ; and there were disorder and plundering among
these gentry which needed suppression.  Lastly, it
was necessary to take some measures for the relief of
the wounded and to detail a small party, both officers
and men, from every regiment which had suffered
heavily, to look after them.  In Brussels the Duke
stayed until the 20th, when he drove over in his
curricle, wearing plain clothes, to join his army at
Nivelles.  The ground was still covered with the dead,
and many French wounded were still lying among
them, who bore their sufferings with admirable patience
and received any help that could be given them with
touching courtesy.

On the night of the 18th Bülow's corps of the
Prussian army halted at Genappe, and Ziethen's on
the Charleroi road a mile or two south of Plancenoit ;
while three brigades of Pirch I.'s corps marched for
Wavre to the assistance of Thielmann.  The last-
named officer had been attacked by Grouchy late in
the afternoon of the 18th, but had held his own
fairly well against odds of two to one until nightfall.
On the 19th, Grouchy, having checked a counter-
attack, pressed Thielmann steadily backward along
the Louvain road until in the course of the forenoon
he heard of the result of the battle of Waterloo,
whereupon he resolved to retreat at once to Namur.
Pirch I., who had reached Mellery on the 19th, pursued

[1] Basil Jackson, *Notes and Reminiscences*, p. 84.
[2] *Ibid.* p. 66.

from thence on the 20th, and Thielmann likewise; 1815. but the French reached Namur with little loss, and June 19. Grouchy, crossing the Meuse, reached Philippeville on the 21st, and went on his way unmolested.

The main armies of Blücher and Wellington marched on the 19th and following days, the former by Charleroi, Avesnes, Etroeung and Fesmy, the latter by Nivelles, Binche and Valenciennes, halting for a day on the 23rd. Le Quesnoi and Valenciennes June 23. were blockaded by Wellington's troops, Landrecies and Maubeuge by the Prussians ; and it was decided by the two commanders to advance to Paris by the right bank of the Oise, as the defeated enemy were said to be assembling at Laon and Soissons. On the 24th Blücher resumed his march, having been joined June 24. by Thielmann's corps, while Wellington halted at Le Cateau to await the arrival of his pontoon-trains. On the 23rd he had detached Colville's division and a few more troops to Cambrai, which had carried the place by escalade with trifling loss ;[1] and the town was set apart for the residence of King Lewis, who had re-entered France from Ghent. On the 26th the June 26. Prussian advanced guard reached Compiègne, and Wellington's army was between Vermand and Péronne. This last place, being fully fortified, refused to surrender ; and the Guards were detached to storm it. The light companies crossed the drawbridge and blew open the gate, whereupon the Governor speedily agreed to a capitulation. On the 27th Grouchy with June 27. a part of his army engaged the Prussians at Compiègne, but, finding himself outnumbered, fell back. He engaged them again on the 28th, and ultimately on June 28. the 29th entered Paris, before the north side of which June 29. the whole of the Prussians encamped that evening. Negotiations for an armistice had already been opened with Wellington by commissioners from the capital, but had been rejected until Napoleon should quit

---

[1] Eight killed, twenty-nine wounded. The troops engaged were the British battalions of Colville's division.

1815.
June 29.
Paris, which on this same day he did. But even so, Paris was not yet taken, and Wellington considered an attack with the forces at his disposal very hazardous.[1] The French troops, with the help of the lines thrown up on the heights from Montmartre to Belleville, could still have checked the advance of the Allies; and it was therefore resolved to send the Prussians round to the south side of the city, which was unfortified.

June 30.
Accordingly on the 30th of June and the two following days the Prussians marched round, not without some sharp fighting both on the 1st and 2nd of July ; Wellington moved his troops into the places

July 3.
vacated by the Prussians ; and on the 3rd, in consequence of overtures from the Provisional Government, a convention was signed under which the Allies agreed to suspend hostilities upon the surrender of Paris, and the French army retired to the Loire.

It was no doubt a relief to Wellington to be quit of the campaign without more fighting, for, if he had thought ill of his army before Waterloo, he thought still worse of it after, when all the best of the men had been killed or disabled. From want of carriages and drivers he could not carry with him one-fourth of the necessary ammunition ; and his staff, its most efficient members having been slain or hurt, was useless. Above all, the behaviour of the Netherlanders, now the greatest part of the army, was infamous. Neither officers nor men would stay with their companies on the march. They wandered from house to house, not excepting Wellington's own head-quarters, robbing, destroying and plundering, forcing the sentries, rescuing the prisoners, and committing every description of outrage. In fact, they were simply a rabble, and for military purposes valueless. Wellington at daybreak of the 26th had ordered a brigade of the Netherlandish infantry to Péronne to support the assault. They arrived at nine o'clock in the evening,

1 Wellington's Despatch to Blücher, 2nd July 1815.

an hour after the Guards had taken the place ; but a 1815.
few Belgian cavalry were on the spot, who, after the
capitulation was signed, cut the ropes of the drawbridge and broke violently into the town. The
British staff-officer, who had arranged the terms,
ordered them out, whereupon the ruffians tried to
cut him down, and the French Governor was actually
obliged to draw his sword to protect him. The
Belgian soldier, properly disciplined and led by good
officers, has deservedly won high reputation on many
fields ; but in 1815 he was neither disciplined nor
controlled, and it is idle to pretend that such levies
were of any military worth. Such incidents as these
prove that the contemporary narratives of Belgian
misbehaviour at Waterloo are absolutely true, and
they are not to be refuted by specious apologies
proffered after the convenient lapse of a century. It
is, however, fair to add that the Prussians behaved as
ill or worse, both before and after the capitulation of
Paris. They had, it is true, old scores to pay off, but
this was no excuse for behaving, as Wellington put it,
like children. " Among the officers of the Allied
troops," he wrote, " the strongest objections are
entertained to anything like discipline and order ";
and this defect caused him not only disgust but not a
little alarm. " If one shot were fired in Paris," he
wrote to Castlereagh on the 14th of July, " the whole
country will rise against us." [1]

On the 6th of July the Prussians occupied Paris, July 6.
while Wellington's army stayed outside. Blücher
wished to levy a huge contribution and, from mere
rage at the name, to blow up the bridge of Jena.
Wellington dissuaded him from the former project
until the Allied Sovereigns should arrive, and meanwhile posted a British sentry on the bridge. This
did not prevent the old Marshal from trying to blow

[1] *Wellington's Despatches.* To Castlereagh, 14th July ; to the
King of the Netherlands, 18th July; to Bathurst and to Sir H. Wellesley,
20th July ; to Torrens, 1st Aug. 1815.

1815. it up, British sentry and all ; but the Prussian engineers failed on the Seine as they had failed on the Sambre from sheer ignorance of their business. And then came the bitter battle of the diplomatists on the terms of peace ; Prussia and the German States clamouring for the dismemberment of France and for a gigantic indemnity ; the Tsar, Castlereagh and Wellington, and later Metternich, standing up strenuously against

Nov. 20. them. On the 20th of November peace was at last signed. France agreed to the cession of Condé, Givet, Charlemont, Philippeville, Mariembourg, Sarrelouis, and Landau, and to the dismantling of Hüningen. The indemnity to be paid by her was fixed at twenty-eight millions sterling ; and it was arranged that for five years an army of one hundred and fifty thousand men [1] should occupy certain places in France at France's expense, the whole being under the command of the Duke of Wellington, with headquarters at Cambrai, for the term of occupation. Martinique and Guadeloupe, which had been occupied in June and August by General Leith, the former bloodlessly, the latter after a little fighting which cost the British about seventy killed and wounded,[2] were both of them restored to France.

So ended this long and desolating war ; and it remains only to recount briefly the fate of some of the principal actors therein, and to review the final campaign. Murat, in a fit of madness, disembarked on the coast of his lost kingdom and was captured and shot on the 13th of October. Ney having been

---

[1] English, Headquarters Cambrai . . . . 30,000
Wurtemburgers, Headquarters Weissenberg . . 5,000
Russians, Headquarters Maubeuge . . . . 30,000
Danes, Headquarters Lewarde . . . . . 5,000
Prussians, Headquarters Sedan . . . . . 30,000
Hanoverians, Headquarters Tourcoing . . . 5,000
Austrians, Headquarters Colmar . . . . 30,000
Saxons, Headquarters Condé . . . . . 5,000
Bavarians, Headquarters Pont-a-Mousson . . 10,000

[2] The troops engaged were the 63rd, York Chasseurs, West India Rangers, and York Rangers. The 63rd had 25 casualties.

arrested and condemned to death, was shot on the 1815.
5th of December. He had sought the honourable
end, that was his due, a thousand times throughout
the long agony of Waterloo ; but the cruel fate
which killed five horses under him reserved the rider
for the bullets of a French firing-party. He lives
immortal as the bravest of the brave. Soult fled
after Waterloo and remained in banishment until
1819, when he began a new career in the service of
France. Of him, as of Marmont and of Victor, we
may perhaps hear again. Masséna, worn out by work
and wounds, died in 1817. He will always be remembered in England as the general who, even in the
years of his decadence, never failed to appear where
Wellington least wanted to see him, and evoked the
unstinted admiration of the entire British army by the
masterly skill of his retreat from before Torres Vedras.

Napoleon himself, after leaving Paris on the 29th
of June, set out for Rochefort with some idea of sailing
for America. He reached the port on the 3rd of July,
and, yielding to the pressure of the Provisional Government, embarked on the 8th. For some days he waited,
forbidden to set foot again in France and yet not
daring to put to sea in face of the British cruisers ;
and on the 13th he wrote his well-known letter of
surrender to the Prince Regent. The original document lies before me as I write, the text in the hand
of some amanuensis, firmly written but containing
one grammatical error, the signature bold and far
more legible than usual, as if to mark with dignity
the close of a transcendently great career. On the
15th he embarked on board the *Bellerophon* and
was carried to Torbay. There had been wild talk
of putting him to death ; and Liverpool wrote flatly
that he wished the King of France would hang or
shoot him, as the best termination of the business ;
but Wellington had no intention of playing the part
of hangman, and the British Government had no idea
of calling upon him to do so. Since, however, it was

1815. necessary for the peace of Europe that he should be kept in safe custody, it fell to England, as practically the only possessor of distant islands and of a fleet that could ensure their safety, to take charge of him. He claimed the right to live quietly in England ; and, a rumour having got abroad that he was to be sent to Fort George at the mouth of the Inverness Firth, the Inverness Local Militia joyfully volunteered to act as his guard.[1] But before the end of July his place of confinement had been determined, and sailing in the King's ship *Northumberland* he landed on the 16th of October at St. Helena.

At the pitiful spectacle of a great genius descending to occupy itself with the pettiest of petty tricks, intrigues, and mischiefs I am not minded even to glance. I have as little wish to study the vast fabric of lies, misstatements, misrepresentations and calumnies that the idle hands at St. Helena took such pains to rear to the honour, as their littleness conceived it, of their royal martyr, and to the shame of his honest and upright custodian. Least of all would I call to remembrance the degrading use to which Whig politicians turned the name, which had made all Europe tremble, to the despicable ends of party strife. It is enough that Napoleon ended his life, by his own choice, without dignity and without resignation. Though a very great captain and a very great administrator, he was always an adventurer and, after his rise to supreme power, always a gambler. From 1803 onward he was continually playing double or quits until he had exhausted the favours of fortune ; and, when she turned against him and all hope was gone, he could not school himself to accept her buffets with a smile. On the 5th of May 1821 the end came, and he was carried to his grave by twelve grenadiers of the Twentieth Foot, no unworthy bearers, for some of them had faced the brave soldiers of

[1] Record Office, H.O. Internal Defence, 322. Lt.-Col. Rose to Sec. of State, 1st Aug. 1815.

Imperial France at Maida, Vimeiro, Coruña, Vitoria,
in the bitterest fights of the Pyrenees, at Orthez and
at Toulouse.


The campaign of Waterloo has been made the
subject of whole libraries of books in all languages,
and has been subjected to examination so microscopic
as to be without parallel in military history. The
reasons are readily found. The story is alluring in
the first place, because it is that of the end of a great
European cataclysm, and because the last act of the
drama brought all the foremost actors of the time
upon the stage. But its greatest attraction is that
it only lasted four days, and may therefore be exhausted
with a comparatively small amount of labour. Whether
the excessive toil expended upon it has really made it
clearer and more intelligible than other campaigns,
may well be doubted. Writers have too. often
approached it with some ulterior object, to illustrate
some theory of war or strategy, to glorify the share
taken by their own nation or even by their own
regiment, to explain the defeat of Napoleon, to
minimise the success of Wellington, to exalt one
commander, to abase another, to prove that, if something had not happened, the result would have been
very different, and so forth. To such mistreatment
many, indeed the majority, have added the mistake of
regarding it as an isolated event, whereas, to take one
detail only, it is impossible for one who has not
deeply studied Graham's campaign of 1814 in the
Netherlands, to understand how bad Wellington's
troops really were. But, after all the study and research
expended upon the four days of the 15th to the 18th
of June 1815, and the new material which it has
produced, it must be confessed that the literature of
Waterloo is more prolific of new conjectures than of
new facts. We know that certain orders were issued
on both sides, and that certain messages were sent and

1815. delivered.   But what other orders or messages, verbal or in writing, may have passed, when the said messages were despatched, when they were delivered, and whether the watches in the French, Prussian, British, and Netherlandish Armies kept uniform time or varied by half - an - hour, we do not know and shall never know.   Wellington warned aspirant historians against inquiring too much, on the ground that such a course would lead to bewilderment rather than truth ; and he was quite right.

The main facts are simple enough.   Napoleon with one hundred and twenty-five thousand men set out to fight Blücher and Wellington with two hundred and fifty thousand.   The two latter had dispersed their armies in cantonments over a very wide front, and Napoleon hoped by stepping in between them to beat them in detail before they could unite, and indeed before either of their armies could be fully concentrated in itself.   The first stage, that is to say, the work of the 15th of June, may be called completely successful. Everything indeed did not pass exactly as Napoleon had designed—that is the rule rather than the exception in war—but it may be said that the British and Prussian commanders were surprised on the 15th. In the details of their concentration bad mistakes were made both by the Prussian staff and by the British commander ;  but the worst mistake of the latter was set right by his Netherlandish subordinates, Constant and Perponcher, who saw the importance of clinging to Quatre Bras.   On the 16th it was Napoleon who was surprised.   He expected to reach Gembloux on one side and Brussels on the other without serious fighting, and he found himself set down to two pitched battles.   It is urged with justice that, if d'Erlon's corps had not been kept walking to and fro all day between the two battle-fields, the issue might have been very different ;  and a vast deal of ingenuity has been expended to account for d'Erlon's conduct.   But the explanation is very simple.   D'Erlon was badly needed upon both battle-fields owing to 1815. the huge initial superiority of the Allies over the French in the matter of numbers. The Emperor had misread the entire situation, and had confused all his commanders by imposing his misreading upon them. Yet even so Napoleon was fortunate in the fact that Blücher chose a bad position and occupied it vilely ; for Ligny, or the equivalent to Ligny, would have resulted very differently if Wellington had been in command of· the Prussian Army. On the other hand, it was unlucky for the Emperor that Wellington was in command at Quatre Bras, for no other General could have handled the early stage of that critical action with such consummate skill, and no troops but the British, fighting under his command, could have made so stubborn a resistance in the face of so heavy punishment.

At nightfall on the 16th, therefore, Napoleon had lost a great number of men and had accomplished very little. The Prussians had indeed·been beaten, but not very severely ; and though ten thousand soldiers of the corps that had suffered most heavily had dispersed, there was one more corps which had been little engaged, and another that had not been engaged at all. It suited Napoleon's preconceived ideas to assume that the Prussians were retreating, without thought of further contest, to the eastward, and that five-and-thirty thousand men would be sufficient, if not to hunt them beyond any sphere of usefulness, at any rate to hold them in check until he should have disposed of Wellington. But here we find the confusion of thought due principally to imperfect intelligence, which vitiated every measure taken by Napoleon after the initial stage of the campaign. Thirty-five thousand were fewer than were necessary to paralyse the Prussians if they were not thoroughly beaten, but more than were necessary to keep them running if they were.

On the French left wing Ney has been much blamed for not attacking Wellington earlier, in order to make

1815. his retreat difficult if not impossible. But it is plain that Ney was thoroughly bewildered by the course which events had taken. An easy, almost unopposed, march to Brussels had been prescribed to him in the first instance, instead of which he had been stopped before he had advanced two miles, and had only been able to hold his ground with great difficulty and serious loss. He could not fail to infer that the Emperor had made grave miscalculations at the very outset of the campaign, that his plans would need revision. The Marshal had received a great many contradictory commands on the 16th, and the general result had not been satisfactory. The Allied armies were, according to Napoleon's design, to have run away in different directions as soon as the French host appeared ; but they had not run away. They had fought desperately, though disunited. One of them had held its ground, and the defeat of the other had not been even reported to Ney until twelve hours after the event. A signal success does not generally take so long to make itself known ; and Ney may well have had his doubts as to the plight of the right wing. There were, in fact, signs of un-certainty and hesitation in the mind of the Commander-in-Chief, easily intelligible in one who had started to fight against an army of twice his own strength, but not calculated to inspire his subordinates with confidence.

The thunderstorm on the 17th was a complication decidedly in favour of the Allies ; but, if we are to go back over past campaigns and alter the weather from day to day, we shall only lose ourselves in unprofitable conjectures. It was open to Napoleon to turn the bulk of his force upon Wellington at Quatre Bras quite early in the morning of the 17th ; and, if he had done so, it is probable that no weather could have saved the campaign from ending very differently. But he did not do so, and when at last he made up his mind to fling himself upon Wellington's rear-guards, it was too late. Meanwhile it is to be noted that the chance of catching Wellington at a disadvantage was due to the neglect of Blücher's staff to apprise the Duke of the Prussian retreat after Ligny. But war is a chapter of accidents ; and any other campaign, if put under the microscope, would show as many as that of Waterloo.

The most remarkable point in the whole story is Wellington's nerve in accepting battle with a very bad army, before he had actually effected his junction with Blücher. It is not impossible that he was prompted thereto by the desire to choose his position for himself and to defend it according to his own ideas, after experience of the Prussian dispositions at Ligny. Yet he took a tremendous risk, for the best of his troops had been very roughly handled at Quatre Bras, and the worst were so bad—not because they were cowards, but because they had no heart in their work —that no reliance could be reposed upon them. The excellent battalions of the German Legion were from the first lamentably weak in numbers ; the best of the British had been very seriously diminished by their losses at Quatre Bras ; and the Hanoverians and Brunswickers, the latter of whom had also suffered considerably, were very young and raw. Altogether, reckoning only the troops which he could trust, more or less, he engaged Napoleon at the odds of two against three. In the matter of guns Napoleon had the advantage of about eight pieces to five in numbers, and of weight of metal into the bargain, for the Emperor, it will be recalled, had several batteries of twelve-pounders, whereas the Duke had nothing heavier than nine-pounders. Everything, therefore, was in Napoleon's favour, except that he was opposed to a strange enemy, whom it pleased him to assume to be similar to all other enemies that he had met. He did not realise that he was matched against a commander who, in the actual direction of a battle, was his equal if not his superior; that the British infantry was as tenacious as the Russian, but far more active and far more formidable with the musket; and that both the

1815. commander and his troops had been well schooled by experience to meet the somewhat crude tactical methods of the French army.

The details of the battle itself, except in its broad lines, are, as usual, so much complicated by conflicting narratives as to defy all attempt to unravel them. It is impossible even to be perfectly sure of the number of battalions of the Imperial Guard which took part in the final attack, much less of their formation and of the portion of the Allied line that was struck by any particular battalion. Only staff-officers can ever catch a general view of any action ; a great number of these were killed or wounded in the course of the day upon both sides, so that they could only give either imperfect narratives or no narratives at all ; and all witnesses agree that the smoke was so dense that the regimental officers always, and the staff-officers for the most part, were working in the dark.

However, Napoleon pursued his usual method of making a great bustle from end to end of his enemy's line, so as to bewilder him as to the true point of the attack ; but it was a new thing to him to fight against an enemy which, as a tactical principle, was kept out of his sight, according (to quote the words of General Foy) to the excellent custom of the English. It may well be, therefore, that he had his own share of bewilderment. Be that as it may, it is certain that his attacks were incoherent—what he would have called *décousus* —though this was a fault which, in general, his worst enemies would have hesitated to attribute to him. We may therefore set down to his subordinates the blunder which converted the advance against Hougoumont from a secondary into a primary operation. But the onslaught of d'Erlon's corps upon the centre, which was really the most serious movement of the whole day, might surely have merited some little personal attention from the General-in-Chief. There were at least three French generals in the field who could have warned Napoleon that an attack upon British

infantry in line by battalions in close column, without 1815.
space to deploy, had again and again been tried and
found wanting. It is true that the assault was finally
routed by a charge of British cavalry ; but this too
might have been foreseen since the day of Salamanca.
There can be little doubt, I think, that this charge had
its effect upon the French infantry all through the day.
Nothing serious was attempted over the scene of the
Union Brigade's attack ; and, according to many
good authorities, the Imperial Guard did not venture
to make its final advance except in squares.

After the failure of d'Erlon, came the great mistake
of attacking unbroken infantry with cavalry only, an
idea which apparently was instilled into the brain of
Ney by the sight of British battalions retiring from the
crest of the hill to the reverse slope. This blunder
on Ney's part and its disastrous consequence must be
placed to the credit of Wellington and of the unseen
array which he alone among his contemporaries
employed when defending a position. Last came the
most trying ordeal of all for the Allies—incessant
raids of cavalry and infantry, sometimes supported by
cannon at close range, and launched at many different
points upon the British squares after a pitiless rain
of shot and shell from Napoleon's massed batteries.
The constancy and steadfastness of British, Hanoverians
and Brunswickers under this trial, especially after
the capture of La Haye Sainte had enabled the French
to enfilade a part of their line, was beyond all praise.
More than one battalion broke, and indeed ran, when
brought into the fighting-line under that terrible fire.
But they rallied and came back ; for, wherever weak-
ness was, there by magic appeared Wellington, perfectly
calm and collected, inspiring all with confidence and
fortitude. He said himself that he personally had
saved the battle four times, and, if he had said forty
times, he would not have overstated the truth. The
men would have been glad enough to advance. What
they found so hard to endure was the incessant fire of

1815. artillery to which they could make no answer. But they were bidden to stand, and, with Wellington to command them, they did stand. The miracles wrought by his presence and personality among a host of raw troops throw into the background the amazing patience and firmness with which, through hours of awful anxiety, he bided his time and forbade any movement until the Prussians should come up. Much is justly made of Blücher's exhortation to his troops to enable him to keep his promise to Wellington. Too little is said and thought of the silent influence and example by which Wellington infused ever fresh courage into a thin line of wavering recruits, and fairly forced them to keep his promise to Blücher. Without his presence and that of the officers and men whom he had taught to meet the legions of France, not only without fear, but with full confidence of victory, Waterloo had been lost.

The final issue of the day was of course decided, as Wellington was the first to acknowledge, by the advent of the Prussians, which was due wholly to the energy of Blücher. With proper management they should have arrived on the field at two ; as things fell out, they did not appear until half-past four and did not make their presence seriously felt until seven. But they won their way through Plancenoit only by strenuous and desperate fighting, which cost them between six and seven thousand killed and wounded and missing. Their casualties, in actual fact, actually exceeded those of the British, strictly so called ; as well they might, for they had many more troops present ;[1] and a comparison of the casualty lists sets forth some curious details. The British officers killed numbered eighty-three, the Prussian twenty-two ; the British officers

[1] The British engaged at Waterloo (*Wellington Supp. Desp.* x. 460-461) numbered 23,991 rank and file, or, adding one-eighth for other ranks, roughly 27,000 men. Bülow's corps at the opening of the campaign numbered 30,000 and Pirch I.'s 31,000. Deducting one-third from these figures as a handsome allowance for casualties and absentees, there are left at least 40,000 men.

wounded three hundred and sixty-three, the Prussian 1815.
two hundred and eighty-six. The tale of the privates
is as follows : killed, of the British twelve hundred and
forty-five, of the Prussians eleven hundred and twenty-
two ; wounded, of the British forty-two hundred and
sixty-one, of the Prussians thirty-eight hundred and
sixty-nine ; missing, of the British five hundred and
fifty-eight, of the Prussians thirteen hundred and five.
These figures do honour to both parties, but leave
little doubt upon whom the brunt of the fighting fell ;
though the credit for one of the most successful
pursuits in military history belongs wholly to the
Prussians, and in particular to Gneisenau.

The losses of the French were appalling. The
only means of judging them are from the published
lists of the fallen officers, which are most pitiful to read.
Never did the French soldier cover himself with
greater glory than at Waterloo, his persistent gallantry
in attack being beyond all praise. The weak point
of the Army was its indiscipline. A large proportion
of the men were old soldiers, very many of them released
prisoners from various countries. They had not had
time to settle down under the rule of their idolised
leader ; and, as they themselves had restored him,
they and the junior officers were inclined to look upon
themselves as the real masters of the situation. The
general officers had many of them reconciled themselves
with the Bourbons. They were sick of war. They
pined for a little peace and quiet and, being of longer
sight than the men, doubted the issue of Napoleon's
usurpation. Thus there was some suspicion in the
lower ranks towards the higher, and no perfect sympathy between them. This probably accounted for
the incoherent nature of the principal attacks both in
general and in detail. If one general hung back,
from reasons of sound military prudence, another in
his heart accused him of treason and hurried him on.
So too in the charges of the French cavalry, every
squadron-leader took matters into his own hands and

1815. attacked upon his own account, fearful lest his colonel
should be lukewarm in the fight ; and thus there was
no grand overwhelming onslaught made at any time
in the day.   Hence, when the Prussians arrived upon
the field in force instead of Grouchy, as the Emperor
had announced, there was a general cry of treachery ;
and the army, saving a few choice regiments, fell
into dissolution.  Discipline was always the weak
side of the Napoleonic armies, and at Waterloo the
defect proved fatal.  None the less the French
approved themselves most noble fighting-men.

There has been much speculation as to the possible
issue of the fight if the Prussians had failed to arrive
on the field.  This is hardly profitable, because
Wellington only accepted battle on the understanding
that Blücher would support him ;  and we have seen
how loyally both chiefs stood by their agreement.
There can be no doubt that many even of the better
Allied troops had been tried almost to the limit of their
endurance, and that there were others besides the
Netherlanders who quitted the field without the
Netherlanders' excuse.  Wellington in a letter to
Lord Mulgrave six months after the battle declared
himself ill-pleased with the conduct of the Artillery,
alleging that, instead of taking refuge in the squares
when the French cavalry charged, they ran off the
field, taking with them limbers, ammunition and
everything.   The Royal Regiment has never forgiven
the Duke for this letter, which indeed seems to be one
of those sweeping indictments to which the great
man was too much prone in moments of impatience.
Whether there was one unfortunate battery which so
misconducted itself, and, if so, which battery it was ;
or whether the whole accusation arose out of some
mistake, some misconception or some misrepresenta-
tion, it is impossible to say.   Wellington averred that,
when the French cavalry fell back, there were no
artillery to fire at them ;  but I can find no evidence
of this, though plenty against it.   Altogether it seems

to me that this letter must be set aside as too hasty to 1815. be accurate.

There was some complaint also of the Light Cavalry on the right wing. Uxbridge rode up to the Guards of Maitland's brigade and said, " Well done, men. By God, we stand on you. If I could only get my fellows to do the same ! But by God, they won't budge—but I'll try again." The writer to whom we owe this detail[1] adds that the Light Cavalry in that part of the field were of little profit, partly because they were brought up for small isolated attacks instead of in a mass. This, however, is quite unconfirmed, rather indeed contradicted, by other authorities ; and it is probable that Uxbridge was speaking of some of the foreign cavalry which, it is well known, refused to follow him. In the infantry, as we have seen, there was at one moment a panic in Halkett's brigade which, however, soon gave place to order. Much has been written about the number of fugitives, chiefly, but by no means exclusively, Nether-landers, that thronged the road to Brussels ; but this is due, I think, to the facts that the number of wounded was very great, and that there was more than the usual number of spectators in the rear of the army. Craufurd had much the same story to tell when he came up to Talavera. On the whole, therefore, I doubt whether the Allies were so much shaken at the close of the battle as French writers have been disposed to think. Up to the very end the French skirmishers tried in vain to tempt the British squares to fire a volley at them which might give a chance to the French battalions to charge while the British muskets were empty. A few picked marksmen alone answered the sharpshooters, and the remainder coolly waited for the word of command to fire.[2] Troops that, after hours

---

[1] MS. Journal of Colonel James Stanhope.

[2] Stanhope tells an amusing story which illustrates the perennial strife between staff-officers and regimental officers. Captain Horace Seymour, one of Uxbridge's aides-de-camp, seeing that the Guards

1815. of harassing attack by all three arms, are still so perfectly under control cannot be considered shaken.

It must be noticed too that, owing to Wellington's admirable husbandry of his reserves, he had still, before the French attacks ceased, Vandeleur's and Vivian's brigades of cavalry, two battalions of Mitchell's brigade of infantry and the Hanoverian brigades of Vincke and Best practically untouched, while the Fourth and Fortieth regiments of Lambert's brigades, the former fresh from work in America, had suffered indeed considerable loss, but nothing so serious as to impair their fighting powers. Colonel James Stanhope, who had exceptionally good opportunities for forming a judgment, thought that even without the Prussians the Allies would have held their ground, and made their final short advance to La Belle Alliance on the 18th ; but he admitted that it was doubtful whether the French or the Allies would have retreated on the 19th. Had Wellington retreated, the Forest of Soignes was easily traversable by troops of all arms, and the border would have made a good defensible position for the rear-guard. Whether Stanhope's opinion were correct or not, it is impossible to say and unprofitable to argue. All that can certainly be said is that, when the battle ended, both armies were rapidly reaching the end of their powers, and that the ammunition of the French artillery was failing.[1] The French had endeavoured at the outset to carry matters forward with a rush, and their failure had cost them very dear. Thenceforward their efforts, though rather more methodical, had still for various reasons continued to be incoherent. The Emperor appears never to have had complete control of the battle ;

---

left the fire of the French skirmishers unanswered, galloped up to Lord Saltoun and said, " G—d d—n you, don't you see those are French ! Why don't you fire at them ? " To which Saltoun replied, " Why, d—n you, don't you think we know better when to fire than you do ! " Seymour thereupon vanished.

[1] *Vie militaire du Général Foy*, p. 281.

and an army, whatever its valour, which goes its own
way in a fight, may collapse suddenly at any moment.
In any case, if the Prussians had not come up and
Napoleon had defeated Wellington, only a very small
fragment of the French army would have been fit for
further work ; and it is questionable whether Napoleon
would have ventured to meet Blücher, who, it may
be presumed, would have made things very unpleasant
for Grouchy. Had the Emperor again engaged the
Prussians, even successfully, he would have been left
with nothing to meet the advance of the main body
of the Allies ; and Paris would have been occupied
in August or September instead of in July.

On the whole it may be said that Napoleon set out
to achieve the impossible, and that his task was so
heavy and so difficult that it was too much even for
his skill and for his powers. It has been pleaded
that he was no longer at his best, and that he was
seriously hampered by the loss of Berthier as the Chief
of his Staff. But no man is always at his best ; and
Wellington was equally without his old and tried
staff-officer, George Murray. Wellington also was
not at his best, otherwise he would not have left sixteen
thousand men at Hal during the battle. This last
matter constitutes a mystery which will never be
cleared up, for Wellington was not the man deliberately
to leave so large a force idle, though within call of the
battlefield, unless there had been some reason which
in his judgment was of overpowering importance.
Blücher and Gneisenau were not at their best, otherwise they would not have accepted battle in so bad a
position as that of Ligny. It may account in part for
their mistakes that not one of the three armies, French,
Prussian and Anglo-German, was really a good one,
all alike having been hastily scraped together, with
imperfect organisation and a large proportion of raw
troops in the ranks. But there were three great
leaders at their head, and under them half-trained
troops became heroes. Napoleon was out-generalled

1815. and out-fought ; but for no other man would the French horse and foot have dashed themselves so incessantly against the line of death on the heights of Mont St. Jean. Blücher's army had been defeated in a very hard fight, and himself, aged seventy-two, ridden over and cruelly battered by galloping squadrons. The old man revived himself partly by strange remedies,[1] more by his own unconquerable spirit, and heartened his men to those superhuman exertions which brought them and their guns, late indeed but in time, to the field of Waterloo.

Lastly, it must be repeated that throughout the long agony of eight terrible hours the Allied line was literally pervaded by Wellington. Wherever danger threatened, there was the thorough - bred chestnut horse and the erect figure in the saddle, wearing the low cocked hat, with the colours of Spain, Portugal and the Netherlands on the cockade, short blue cloak over a blue frock-coat and white leathers—the keen grey eyes always alert, the mouth inflexibly firm, and the expression unchangeably serene. Now he was heartening some hardly-pressed British battalion, now rallying some broken auxiliaries, now leading some young Hanoverians from the second line into the first ; and in the lulls, when the musketry was silent and the French artillery was tearing up the front, he would send his staff to the reverse slope and, attended by one officer only, would stand in the full tempest of shot and shell gazing at the French troops on the other side of the valley. He was one who was never demonstrative in any circumstances, who said little and was sparing of gesture. But his mere presence diffused an atmosphere of calm and confidence, and all who were aware of it thanked God and took courage. His eye too was everywhere.

---

[1] He dosed himself with gin and onions ; and on approaching Hardinge directly afterwards observed, no doubt with truth, " Ich stinke etwas." Stanhope. *Conversations of the Duke of Wellington,* p. 101.

It caught sight of a French gun-carriage flying to 1815. splinters under the blow of an English shot ; and away flew an aide-de-camp to place under arrest the commander of a battery who had dared to fire at guns when the order was to fire only at men. Without Wellington the Allied line could never have endured to the end, and he was in a modest way aware of it. " It has been a damned nice thing," he told Creevey next day, " the nearest run thing that ever you saw in your life. By God," he added, as if thinking aloud, " I don't think it would have done if I had not been there."

The Prince of Orange on the morrow of the fight wrote anxiously to the Duke " to know how he could explain or pass over the conduct of the Netherlands' troops." The Duke answered, " I shall praise generally and not in detail, so nobody will know anything about them." There was glory enough, he said later, for every one, and he spoke truly. There was not a nation among the Allies which had not at one period or another rendered transcendent service to the cause of Europe in that short campaign ; and not one that had fought more valiantly than their most noble and gallant enemy. Had Waterloo not been a final and decisive battle, it would have been coupled with Albuera in the popular memory as a great feat of endurance and tenacity. But, though its fame may be partly obscured by later and more gigantic contests, it can never be wholly obliterated. Napoleons do not so frequently appear that the downfall of them and of the power that they have wielded can readily lose significance. By a happy coincidence it occurred simultaneously to the Commanders-in-Chief in the field and at the Horse Guards that so heroic a fight and so momentous an occasion should be commemorated, for the first time since Dunbar, by the issue of a medal to every man in the army who had been present ; and this medal is still the possession most highly treasured alike in the highest and the humblest of English homes.

1815. The design is of little merit, yet it is unique, and worthily unique, among British military medals, for it bears on the reverse, besides the name and date of the battle, the name of him without whom there would have been no victory—the one word Wellington.

# APPENDIX I

## THE ANGLO-ALLIED ARMY IN THE WATERLOO CAMPAIGN

*Commander-in-Chief.*—Field-Marshal the Duke of Wellington, K.G.
*Quarter-master-General.*—Colonel Oliver De Lancey.

(G.) signifies regiments that had served with Graham in the Netherlands; (P.) regiments that had served in the Peninsular War.

### First Corps (The Prince of Orange)

First Division (Maj.-Gen. Cooke).

| | |
|---|---|
| 1st British Brigade Maj.-Gen. Maitland | 2/1st Guards (G.)<br>3/1st Guards |
| 2nd British Brigade Maj.-Gen. Sir John Byng | 2nd Coldstream Guards (G.)<br>2/3rd Guards (G.) |

*Artillery*—Sandham's British and Kuhlmann's K.G.L. field-batteries.

Total—4061 infantry, 12 guns.

Third Division (Lieut.-Gen. Sir Charles Alten).

| | |
|---|---|
| 5th British Brigade Maj.-Gen. Sir Colin Halkett | 2/30th (G.), 33rd (G.)<br>2/69th (G.), 2/73rd (G.) |
| 2nd K.G.L. Brigade Col. von Ompteda | 1st and 2nd Light Battalions K.G.L.<br>5th and 8th Line Battalions K.G.L. |
| 1st Hanoverian Brigade Maj.-Gen. Count Kielmansegge | 6 Hanoverian battalions |

*Artillery*—Lloyd's British and Cleeves's K.G.L. field-batteries.

Total—6970 infantry, 12 guns.

213

Second Netherlandish Division (Lieut.-Gen. Baron de Perponcher).

1st Brigade
    Maj.-Gen. de Bijlandt } 5 Netherlandish battalions
2nd Brigade
    Prince Bernard of Saxe- } 5 Nassau battalions
    Wiemar

*Artillery*—One field-battery, Bijleveld's horse-battery.

Total—7700 infantry, 12 guns.

Third Netherlandish Division (Lieut.-Gen. Baron de Chassé).

1st Brigade
    Maj.-Gen. Detmers } 6 Netherlandish battalions
2nd Brigade
    Maj.-Gen. d'Aubremé } 6 Netherlandish battalions

*Artillery*—A field-battery and a horse-battery, Netherlandish.

Total—6669 infantry, 16 guns.

TOTAL FIRST CORPS—25,400 infantry, 56 guns.

SECOND CORPS (Lieut.-Gen. Lord Hill)

Second Division (Lieut.-Gen. Sir H. Clinton).

3rd British Brigade
    Maj.-Gen. Adam } 1/52nd (P.), 1/71st (P.)
                     2/95th (P.), 3/95th (G.)
1st K.G.L. Brigade
    Col. Du Plat } 1st, 2nd, 3rd, 4th Line Battalions
                   K.G.L.
3rd Hanoverian Brigade
    Col. Hew Halkett } 4 Landwehr battalions

*Artillery*—Bolton's British and Sympher's K.G.L. field-batteries.

Total—6833 infantry, 12 guns.

Fourth Division (Lieut.-Gen. Sir C. Colville).

4th British Brigade
    Col. Mitchell } 3/14th, 1/23rd (P.), 51st (P.)
6th British Brigade
    Maj.-Gen. Johnstone } 2/35th (G.), 1/54th (G.)
                          59th, 1/91st (G.)
6th Hanoverian Brigade
    Maj.-Gen. Sir James } 5 Hanoverian battalions
    Lyon

*Artillery*—Brome's British and Rettberg's Hanoverian field-batteries.

Total—7217 infantry, 12 guns.

Corps of Prince Frederick of the Netherlands.

1st Netherlandish Division } D'Hauw's Brigade, 6 battalions
Lieut.-Gen. Stedman } De Eerens's Brigade, 5 battalions

Total—6437 infantry, and one field-battery of 8 guns.

Anthing's Netherland
Indian Brigade } 5 battalions and 1 field-battery

Total—3499 infantry, 8 guns.

TOTAL SECOND CORPS—23,986 infantry, 40 guns.

CAVALRY

1st Brigade
  Maj.-Gen. Lord E. } 1st and 2nd Life Guards, Blues
  Somerset
2nd Brigade
  Maj.-Gen. Sir W. } Royals, Greys, Inniskillings
  Ponsonby
3rd Brigade
  Maj.-Gen. Sir W. } 1st and 2nd Light Dragoons K.G.L.
  Dörnberg } 23rd Light Dragoons
4th Brigade
  Maj.-Gen. Sir J. } 11th, 12th, 16th Light Dragoons
  Vandeleur
5th Brigade
  Maj.-Gen. Sir } 7th and 15th Hussars
  Colquhoun Grant } 2nd Hussars K.G.L.
6th Brigade
  Maj.-Gen. Sir Hussey } 10th and 18th Hussars
  Vivian } 1st Hussars K.G.L.
7th Brigade } 13th Light Dragoons
  Col. Arentschild } 3rd Hussars K.G.L.

*Artillery* — Bull's (howitzers), Gardiner's, Mercer's, Ramsay's, Webler-Smith's, and Whinyates's horse-batteries.

Total—8471 cavalry, 36 guns.

1st Hanoverian Cavalry
  Brigade } 3 regiments, 1682 men

Brunswick Cavalry } 1 regiment and 1 squadron, 922 cavalry

Netherlandish Cavalry } 3 brigades (Trip, de Ghigny, Van Merlen), 7 regiments, and 2 half-batteries

Total—3405 cavalry and 8 guns.

TOTAL CAVALRY—14,482 and 44 guns.

GARRISONS

Seventh Division.

7th British Brigade   } 2/25th (G.), 2/37th (G.), 2/78th (G.)
                         3 British garrison battalions.

Total—3233 men.

Hanoverian Reserve Corps   12 Landwehr battalions in 4 brigades
Total—9000 men.

TOTAL GARRISONS—12,233 men.

GRAND TOTAL (including 1240 Engineers and waggon-train)—
105,834 men and 204 guns.


RESERVE

Fifth Division (Lieut-Gen. Sir Thomas Picton).

8th British Brigade
  Maj.-Gen. Sir James   } 1/28th (P.), 1/32nd (P.)
  Kempt                   1/79th (P.), 1/95th (P.)
9th British Brigade
  Maj.-Gen. Sir Denis   } 3/1st (P.), 1/42nd (P.)
  Pack                    2/44th (P.), 1/92nd (P.)
5th Hanoverian Brigade
  Col. von Vincke       } 4 Landwehr battalions

*Artillery*—Rogers's British and Braun's Hanoverian field-batteries.
Total—7158 infantry, 12 guns.

Sixth Division.

10th British Brigade
  Maj.-Gen. Sir John    } 1/4th (P.)., 1/27th (P.)
  Lambert                 1/40th (P.), 2/81st (P.)
4th Hanoverian Brigade
  Col. Best             } 4 Landwehr battalions

*Artillery*—Unett's and Sinclair's field-batteries.
Total—5149 infantry, 12 guns.


British Reserve Artillery.

  2 horse-batteries (Ross and Bean).
  3 field-batteries (Morisson, Hutchesson, Ilbert).


Brunswick Corps (The Duke of Brunswick).

  Advanced guard, 4 companies infantry, detachment cavalry, 2
  brigades (each 3 battalions), and 2 batteries.
Total—5376 infantry and 16 guns.

Nassau Contingent (General von Kruse), 3 battalions.
Total—2841 infantry.

TOTAL RESERVE—20,524 infantry, 64 guns.

## TOTAL STRENGTH BY NATIONALITIES

| Nation. | Infantry. | | Cavalry. | | Guns. |
|---|---|---|---|---|---|
| British . . | . 20,310 rank and file | | 5,911 rank and file | | 90 |
| K.G.L. . | . 3,285 ,, | ,, | 2,560 ,, | ,, | 18 |
| Hanoverians . | . 13,793 ,, | ,, | 1,682 ,, | ,, | 12 |
| Brunswick . | . 5,376 ,, | ,, | 922 ,, | ,, | 16 |
| Nassau . . | . 7,308 all ranks | | ... | | ... |
| Netherlanders | . 18,838 ,, | | 3,405 all ranks | | 56 |
| | 68,910 | | 14,480 | | 192 |

(Taken from *The Campaign of 1815*, by Lieut.-Col. W. H. James.)

# APPENDIX II

## STRENGTH OF THE BRITISH ARMY PRESENT AT WATERLOO

(Abridged from the Field-State printed by Siborne, which, however, seems from internal evidence to be imperfect.)

| Division | Brigade | Regiments | Officers | Other ranks |
|---|---|---|---|---|
| | | R.A. | 175 | 4769 |
| | | K.G.L. Art. | 25 | 546 |
| | | R.E. | 37 | ... |
| | | Sappers & Miners | 10 | 735 |
| | | Waggon-Train | 16 | 285 |
| | | Staff Corps | 18 | 251 |
| Cav. | 1st | 1st L.G. | 16 | 229 |
| | | 2nd L.G. | 20 | 215 |
| | | Blues | 19 | 232 |
| | | K.D.G. | 29 | 568 |
| | 2nd | 1st. D. | 30 | 398 |
| | | 2nd D. | 28 | 414 |
| | | 6th D. | 26 | 419 |
| | 3rd | 1st L.D.K.G.L. | 34 | 500 |
| | | 2nd L.D.K.G.L. | 33 | 472 |
| | | 23rd L.D. | 28 | 313 |
| | 4th | 11th L.D. | 27 | 408 |
| | | 12th L.D. | 26 | 401 |
| | | 16th L.D. | 30 | 403 |
| | 5th | 7th Hrs. | 18 | 344 |
| | | 15th Hrs. | 28 | 419 |
| | | 2nd Hrs. K.G.L. | 36 | 547 |
| | 6th | 10th Hrs. | 26 | 426 |
| | | 18th Hrs. | 25 | 417 |
| | | 1st Hrs. K.G.L. | 36 | 550 |
| | | 13th L.D. | 28 | 420 |
| | | 3rd Hrs. K.G.L. | 37 | 647 |

| Division | Brigade | Regiments | Officers | Other ranks |
|---|---|---|---|---|
| | | INFANTRY. | | |
| 1st | 1st Brit. | 2/1st Gds. | 29 | 752 |
| | | 3/1st Gds. | 29 | 818 |
| | 2nd Brit. | 2/C. Gds. | 36 | 1006 |
| | | 2/3rd Gds. | 34 | 1021 |
| 3rd | 5th Brit. | 2/30th | 40 | 593 |
| | | 1/33rd | 31 | 535 |
| | | 2/69th | 30 | 511 |
| | | 2/73rd | 23 | 475 |
| | 2nd K.G.L. | 5th Line K.G.L. | 31 | 471 |
| | | 8th Line K.G.L. | 32 | 513 |
| | | 1st Light K.G.L. | 32 | 458 |
| | | 2nd Light K.G.L. | 31 | 406 |
| 2nd | 3rd Brit. | 1/52nd | 59 | 1079 |
| | | 1/71st | 50 | 931 |
| | | Det. 3/95th | 10 | 193 |
| | | 2/95th | 34 | 621 |
| | 1st K.G.L. | 1st Line K.G.L. | 29 | 426 |
| | | 2nd Line K.G.L. | 29 | 463 |
| | | 3rd Line K.G.L. | 30 | 553 |
| | | 4th Line K.G.L. | 30 | 448 |
| 5th | 4th Brit. | 3/14th | 38 | 592 |
| | | 1/23rd | 44 | 697 |
| | | 1/51st | 45 | 474 |
| | 8th Brit. | 1/28th | 35 | 521 |
| | | 1/32nd | 26 | 477 |
| | | 1/79th | 26 | 414 |
| | | 1/95th | 17 | 401 |
| | 9th Brit. | 3/1st | 36 | 417 |
| | | 1/42nd | 17 | 312 |
| | | 2/44th | 20 | 450 |
| | | 1/92nd | 22 | 400 |
| | 10th Brit. | 1/4th | 27 | 643 |
| | | 1/27th | 21 | 729 |
| | | 1/40th | 43 | 819 |

# APPENDIX III

## COMPOSITION OF THE PRUSSIAN ARMY UNDER FIELD-MARSHAL PRINCE VON BLÜCHER

*Chief of Staff.*—Lieut.-General Count von Gneisenau.
*Quarter-master-General.*—Major-General von Grolmann.

### Ist Army Corps (Lieut.-Gen. von Ziethen)

| | | | | |
|---|---|---|---|---|
| 1st Brigade | Steinmetz | 9069 men | 16 guns |
| 2nd ,, | Pirch II. | 8018 ,, | 18 ,, |
| 3rd ,, | Jagow | 7146 ,, | 8 ,, |
| 4th ,, | Henckel | 4900 ,, | 8 ,, |
| Reserve Cavalry | Röder | 2175 ,, | 8 ,, |
| Reserve Artillery | Rentzell | | 30 ,, |

Total Ist Corps—31,308 men, 88 guns.

### IInd Army Corps (Gen. von Pirch I.)

| | | | | |
|---|---|---|---|---|
| 5th Brigade | Tippelskirch | 7153 men | 8 guns |
| 6th ,, | Krafft | 6762 ,, | 8 ,, |
| 7th ,, | Brause | 6503 ,, | 8 ,, |
| 8th ,, | Bose | 6584 ,, | 8 ,, |
| Reserve Cavalry | Wahlen | 4471 ,, | 8 ,, |
| Reserve Artillery | | | 32 ,, |

Total IInd Corps—31,473 men, 72 guns.

### IIIrd Army Corps (Lieut.-Gen. von Thielmann)

| | | | | |
|---|---|---|---|---|
| 9th Brigade | Borcke | 7262 men | 8 guns |
| 10th ,, | Kemphen | 4419 ,, | 8 ,, |
| 11th ,, | Lück | 3980 ,, | 8 ,, |
| 12th ,, | Stulpnagel | 6614 ,, | 8 ,, |
| Reserve Cavalry | Hobe | 1981 ,, | 8 ,, |
| Reserve Artillery | Grevenitz | | 16 ,, |

Total IIIrd Corps—24,256 men, 56 guns.

### IVᴛʜ Corps (Gen. Count Bülow)

| | | | | |
|---|---|---|---|---|
| 13th Brigade . | . Hake . . . | 6560 men | 8 guns |
| 14th ,, . | . Ryssel . . . | 7138 ,, | 8 ,, |
| 15th ,, . | . Losthin . . . | 7143 ,, | 8 ,, |
| 16th ,, . | . Hiller . . . | 6423 ,, | 8 ,, |
| Reserve Cavalry . | Prince William . | 3321 ,, | 16 ,, |
| Reserve Artillery . | Bardeben . . . . | | 32 ,, |

Total IVth Corps—30,585 men, 80 guns.

### SUMMARY

| | | | |
|---|---|---|---|
| Ist Corps . . . | 27,817 infantry | 2,675 cavalry | 88 guns |
| IInd Corps . . | 25,836 ,, | 4,471 ,, | 72 ,, |
| IIIrd Corps . . | 20,611 ,, | 2,581 ,, | 56 ,, |
| IVth Corps . . | 25,381 ,, | 3,921 ,, | 80 ,, |
| Total . . | 99,645 ,, | 13,648 ,, | 296 ,, |

(exclusive of gunners, engineers, and train.)

(Abstracted from Appendix to *The Campaign of 1815*, by
Lieut-Col. W. H. James.)

# APPENDIX IV

## COMPOSITION OF THE FRENCH ARMY UNDER THE EMPEROR NAPOLEON

*Chief of Staff.*—Marshal Soult, Duke of Dalmatia.

### IMPERIAL GUARD (DROUOT)

*Infantry.*

|  | Men. |
|---|---|
| Friant—1st, 2nd, 3rd, 4th Grenadiers . . . . | 4,140 |
| Morand—1st, 2nd, 3rd, 4th Chasseurs . . . . | 4,603 |
| Duhesme—1st, 2nd Tirailleurs, 1st, 2nd Voltigeurs . | 4,283 |
| Total Infantry . . . | 13,026 |

*Cavalry.*

Lefebvre Desnoëttes—Lancers and Mounted Chasseurs  
Guyot—Dragoons and Horse Grenadiers . . } 4100  
D'Autancourt—Gendarmerie d'Élite . . .

*Artillery.*

Desvaux—13 foot- and 3 horse-batteries.
Engineers and sailors of the Guard.

Total—20,755 men, 122 guns.

### FIRST CORPS D'ARMÉE (D'ERLON)

| First Division. Quiot. | ? Brigade, 54th, 55th Line<br>Bourgeois's Brigade, 28th, 105th Line | } 4000 |
|---|---|---|
| Second Division. Douzelot. | Schmitz's Brigade, 13th Light, 17th Line<br>Aulard's Brigade, 19th, 51st Line | } 5132 |
| Third Division. Marcognet. | Noguez's Brigade, 21st, 46th Line<br>Grenier's Brigade, 25th, 45th Line | } 3900 |

Men.

| Fourth Division. Durutte. | Pégot's Brigade, 8th, 29th Line<br>Brue's Brigade, 58th, 95th Line | }3853 |

| First Cavalry Division. Jacquinot. | Bruno's Brigade   }3rd Chass., 7th Hussars<br>Gobrecht's Brigade }3rd, 4th Lancers | }1706 |

*Artillery*—5 foot-batteries, 1 horse-battery.
*Engineers*—5 companies.

Total (with train)—20,731 men, 46 guns.

### Second Corps d'Armée (Reille)

| Fifth Division. Bachelu. | Husson's Brigade, 2nd Light, 61st Line<br>Campy's Brigade, 72nd, 108th Line | }4103 |

| Sixth Division. Jérôme Bonaparte. | Bauduin's Brigade, 1st, 3rd Light<br>Soye's Brigade, 1st, 2nd Line | }7819 |

| Seventh Division. Girard. | Devilliers's Brigade, 11th Light, 82nd Line<br>Piat's Brigade, 12th Light, 4th Line | }3925 |

| Ninth Division. Foy. | Gauthier's Brigade, 92nd, 93rd Line<br>B. Jamin's Brigade, 4th Light, 100th Line | }4788 |

| Second Cavalry Division. Piré. | Huberts's Brigade, 1st, 6th Chasseurs<br>Vathiez's Brigade, 5th, 6th Lancers | }2064 |

*Artillery*—5 foot-batteries, 1 horse-battery.
*Engineers*—5 companies.

Total (with train)—25,179 men, 46 guns.

### Third Corps d'Armée (Vandamme)

| Eighth Division. Lefol. | Billard's Brigade, 15th Light, 23rd Line<br>Corsin's Brigade, 37th, 64th Line | }4541 |

| Tenth Division. Habert. | Gengoux's Brigade, 34th, 88th Line<br>Dupeyroux's Brigade, 22nd, 70th Line<br>2nd Swiss Foreign Legion | }5024 |

Men.

Eleventh Division. Berthezène.
{ Dufour's Brigade, 12th, 56th Line
Lagarde's Brigade, 33rd, 86th Line }5565

Third Cavalry Division. Domont.
{ Dommanget's Brigade, 4th, 9th Chasseurs
Vinot's Brigade, 12th Chasseurs }1017

*Artillery*—4 foot-batteries, 1 horse-battery.

*Engineers*—3 companies.

Total (with train)—18,105 men, 46 guns.


### Fourth Corps d'Armée (Gérard)

Twelfth Division. Pécheux.
{ Romme's Brigade, 30th, 96th Line
Schœffer's Brigade, 6th Light, 63rd Line }4719

Thirteenth Division. Vichéry.
{ Le Capitaine's Brigade, 59th, 76th Line
Desprez's Brigade, 48th, 60th Line }4145

Fourteenth Division. Bourmont.
{ Hulot's Brigade, 9th Light, 11th Line
Toussaint's Brigade, 44th, 50th Line }4237

Seventh Cavalry Division. Maurin.
{ Vallin's Brigade, 6th Hussars, 8th Chasseurs
Berruyer's Brigade, 6th, 16th Dragoons }1500

*Artillery*—5 foot-batteries, 1 horse-battery.

*Engineers*—3 companies.

Total (with train)—16,219 men, 46 guns.


### Sixth Corps d'Armée (Lobau)

Nineteenth Division. Simmer.
{ Bellair's Brigade, 5th, 11th Line
M. Jamin's Brigade, 27th, 84th Line }3953

Twentieth Division. Jannin.
{ Bony's Brigade, 5th Light, 10th Line
Tromelin's Brigade, 47th, 107th Line }2202

Men.

Twenty-first
Division.
Teste.
{ Lafitte's Brigade, 8th Light, 40th Line
Penne's Brigade, 65th, 75th Line } 2418

*Artillery*—4 foot-batteries.

*Engineers*—3 companies.

Total (with train)—10,821 men, 32 guns.

## Reserve Cavalry (Marshal Grouchy)

### First Cavalry Corps (Pajol)

Fourth
Cavalry
Division.
P. Soult.
{ St. Laurent's Brigade }
Ameil's Brigade } 1st, 4th, 5th Hussars

Fifth
Cavalry
Division.
Subervie.
{ A. de Colbert's Brigade, 1st, 2nd Lancers
Merlin's Brigade, 11th Chasseurs } 2536

*Artillery*—2 horse-batteries.

### Second Cavalry Corps (Exelmans)

Ninth
Cavalry
Division.
Strolz.
{ Burthe's Brigade, 5th, 13th Dragoons
Vincent's Brigade, 15th, 20th Dragoons }

Tenth
Cavalry
Division.
Chastel.
{ Bonnemains's Brigade, 4th, 12th Dragoons
Berton's Brigade, 14th, 17th Dragoons } 3116

*Artillery*—2 horse-batteries.

### Third Cavalry Corps (Kellermann)

Eleventh
Cavalry
Division.
l'Héritier.
{ Piquet's Brigade, 2nd, 7th Dragoons
Guiton's Brigade, 8th, 11th Cuirassiers }

Twelfth
Cavalry
Division.
Roussel
d'Harbal.
{ Blancard's Brigade, 1st, 2nd Carbineers
Donop's Brigade, 2nd, 3rd Cuirassiers } 3400

*Artillery*—2 horse-batteries.

### Fourth Cavalry Corps (Milhaud)

Men.

| | | |
|---|---|---|
| Thirteenth Cavalry Division. Wathier. | Dubois's Brigade, 1st, 4th Cuirassiers<br>Travers's Brigade, 7th, 12th Cuirassiers | |
| Fourteenth Cavalry Division. Delort. | Farine's Brigade, 5th, 10th Cuirassiers<br>Vial's Brigade, 6th, 9th Cuirassiers | 2797 |

*Artillery*—2 horse-batteries.

Total Reserve Cavalry—11,849 men (without train), 48 guns.

### SUMMARY

| | Infantry. | Cavalry. | Artillery. | Engineers, etc. | Guns. |
|---|---|---|---|---|---|
| Imperial Guard . . | 13,026 | 4,100 | 2,786 | 109 | 122 |
| 1st Corps d'Armée . | 16,885 | 1,706 | 1,096 | 330 | 46 |
| 2nd ,, ,, . | 20,635 | 2,064 | 1,700 | 409 | 46 |
| 3rd ,, ,, . | 15,130 | 1,017 | 1,084 | 146 | 38 |
| 4th ,, ,, . | 13,401 | 1,500 | 1,417 | 201 | 38 |
| 6th ,, ,, . | 8,573 | ... | 765 | 189 | 32 |
| Reserve Cavalry . . | ... | 11,849 | 1,222 | ... | 48 |
| Total . . | 87,650 | 22,236 | 10,070 | 1,384 | 370 |

Grand Total (including train)—124,139 men, 370 guns.

(Abridged from Appendix to *The Campaign of 1815*, by Lieut.-Col. W. H. James.)

# INDEX

King's Dragoon.